Born to Bloom

"Author La Vonne Earl's new release, *Born to Bloom*, is an amazing tool for emotional healing. If you or someone you know is suffering from the consequences of sexual abuse or abuse in general, this is your book. It will guide you through the steps to a life of freedom, emotional wholeness and happiness.

Where traditional methods of counseling have failed, La Vonne's workbook has been successful to lead many out of their lifelong struggles. Her steps to wholeness reflect on who God has created you to be, helping you to discover your life goals and purposes. La Vonne's methods for healing have proved to be very successful because she's based it on the tried-and-true foundation of the Word of God. And as a Master Certified Christian Coach, she's had ample opportunity to use it to walk the wounded from a place of pain into the embrace of Father God and their position as His beloved child."

Candice Simmons
Passion & Fire Ministries

"*Born to Bloom* helped me to let go of so much pain and see my future with hope. I now feel like I am no different than anyone else, as I have discovered I am loved regardless of what has happened to me. I want to give back and help others find their healing as well."

Sarah

"After being abused, I didn't feel like I could live another day. I hated my life and myself. After going through *Born to Bloom*, I now feel like I can handle my emotions and feelings. I have learned how to reprogram my mind to work for me and not against me anymore. I now have an understanding on how to evaluate myself, set new goals and surround myself with the right people so that I can live the good life that I have always dreamed about. I have learned that I do not have to repeat the same patterns of dysfunction. I am happier and more at peace."

Anonymous

"La Vonne writes this book as if she is with the person who is reading. She had me hooked when she included Sabbath rest as critical to total health. We have a tendency to reward busyness; wounded people often become "too busy working on our issues." La Vonne uses keen biblical insight to explain God's rest. She emphasizes the necessity of daily quiet time, scripture memorization, awareness, inner narrative development, accountability, applications in peripheral areas, wholeness, and more.

As in her book *A Coach for Christ*, La Vonne provides a plethora of appendices. There is a multitude of biblical references to help with knowing God's love. There are also many "Who I am in Christ" statements to help transform your inner narrative. I am already using this text to improve my knowledge and skills as a Chaplain. I highly recommend this workbook as a valuable resource for group healing."

Reverend Houston R. Jr.

Born to Bloom

Complete Healing from Any Form of Sexual Abuse

La Vonne Earl

Like the lotus flower, rising above and being made new through Christ power within.

Born to Bloom: Complete Healing From Any Form of Sexual Abuse
Copyright ©2021 by La Vonne Earl

All rights reserved. This book or any portion thereof may not be reproduced or used in any manner whatsoever without the express written permission of the publisher except for the use of brief quotations in a book review.

YKI coaching
www.YKIcoachingcom

Book Design: Carla Green, Clarity Designworks

Paperback ISBN 978-0-9855382-0-0
Ebook ISBN 978-0-9855382-2-4

Scripture quotations marked (BSB) are taken from The Holy Bible, Berean Study Bible, BSB Copyright © 2016, 2018 by Bible Hub. Used by permission. All rights reserved worldwide.

Scripture quotations marked (CEB) are taken from the COMMON ENGLISH BIBLE. © Copyright 2011 COMMON ENGLISH BIBLE. All rights reserved. Used by permission. (www.CommonEnglishBible.com).

Scripture quotations marked (ERV) are taken from the Holy Bible: Easy-to-Read Version (ERV), International Edition © 2013, 2016 by Bible League International and used by permission.

Scripture quotations marked (ESV) are taken from the *ESV® Bible (The Holy Bible, English Standard Version®)*, copyright © 2001 by Crossway, a publishing ministry of Good News Publishers. Used by permission. All rights reserved.

Scripture quotations marked (KJV) are taken from the King James Version of the Bible.

Scripture quotations marked (MSG) are taken from *THE MESSAGE*, copyright © 1993, 2002, 2018 by Eugene H. Peterson. Used by permission of NavPress. All rights reserved. Represented by Tyndale House Publishers, a Division of Tyndale House Ministries.

Scripture quotations marked (NASB) are taken from the NEW AMERICAN STANDARD BIBLE®, Copyright © 1960, 1962,1963,1968,1971,1972,1973,1975,1977,1995 by The Lockman Foundation. Used by permission.

Scripture quotations marked (NET Bible) are taken from the NET Bible® (http://netbible.com), copyright ©1996, 2019 used with permission from Biblical Studies Press, L.L.C. All rights reserved.

Scripture quotations marked (NKJV) are taken from the New King James Version®. Copyright © 1982 by Thomas Nelson. Used by permission. All rights reserved.

Scripture quotations marked (NIV) are taken from the *Holy Bible, New International Version®, NIV®*. Copyright © 1973, 1978, 1984, 2011 by Biblica, Inc.™ Used by permission of Zondervan. All rights reserved worldwide. www.zondervan.com. The "NIV" and "New International Version" are trademarks registered in the United States Patent and Trademark Office by Biblica, Inc.™

Scripture quotations marked (NLT) are taken from the *Holy Bible, New Living Translation*, copyright ©1996, 2004, 2015 by Tyndale House Foundation. Used by permission of Tyndale House Publishers, a Division of Tyndale House Ministries, Carol Stream, Illinois 60188. All rights reserved.

Scripture quotations marked (TPT) are taken from *The Passion Translation®*. Copyright © 2017, 2018 by Passion & Fire Ministries, Inc. Used by permission. All rights reserved. ThePassionTranslation.com.

NOTE: All names in any stories told, and some details of the stories, have been changed to protect the identities of those involved.

Contents

Foreword 9

Acknowledgments 11

How to Use This Book 13

Introduction 19

Week 1: You Are Not Alone 21

Week 2: Choosing to Heal 51

Week 3: Getting to Know the Real You 69

Week 4: Getting to Know Your Boundaries 91

Week 5: Changing Your Mindset 119

Week 6: Loving Yourself — Body, Mind & Spirit 143

Week 7: Putting It All Together 161

Conclusion 177

Appendix 179

Foreword

I met La Vonne many years ago when we toured a local mission together. After our tour, we sat to have lunch at a table in the sunlit courtyard of the facility. As we ate, I listened to her share about her love for helping others and her heart for reaching people who have been affected by abuse. I knew then that we would become friends and fellow workers in our own missions to help others find hope, when it seems like there is none.

I took a training course through her Christian Coaching model and experienced firsthand La Vonne's gift for effectively leading others to use their God-given talents to coach and support hurting people. Her method of teaching and sharing includes the process of learning to develop rapport, listen effectively, and easily communicate. She is a master in all three of these areas. With the right tools and resources and above all, the love of God, we can all be healed and whole. Psalm 147:3 tells us, "He heals the brokenhearted and binds up their wounds." We come to this work as women who have experienced the darkness of being mistreated and misused, and as women who understand that while our pain cannot be compared, it can be understood, and it can be overcome.

La Vonne's practical approach to healing and wholeness is something we can all use. She is skilled and equipped and it shows in the core teachings she lays out in this workbook, all of which are necessary for a balanced and productive life. In this workbook she takes us on a journey of self-introspection and truth seeking. You will learn how to set goals, make plans and surround yourself with the right people to hold you accountable. Often, the process of self-examination and revisiting past hurts can be painful, but this is so different in that it provides an optimistic and practical way to build your future.

I loved revisiting the concepts I learned through her training that reminded me of the necessity to pay attention to the "Six Key Areas of Life." La Vonne guides the reader through these areas to help them overcome and find new hope for their future. I would encourage you to approach this workbook as an expedition to a bright new beginning. La Vonne is someone who models what she believes and knows with perseverance we can become mature and complete to live the life God intended for us. And the good news is that He wants us to have a life filled with love, joy and peace!

One of the things I really liked working on in this book is the Daily Healing Activities. The habit of memorizing scriptures and honestly answering the questions posed is an exercise that will serve you well now and, in the future, as you continually seek to work on the key areas of your life. I also found the section on boundaries particularly relevant for those of us who have experienced abuse. When we are violated in a way that causes us trauma and hurt, the ability to see the lines that should not be crossed can become blurred. La Vonne helps to make those lines clear and helps the reader understand the necessity to implement healthy boundaries in all areas of life.

I have been through the healing process myself. I knew that my life had to change dramatically if I was going to survive in this world. I cannot tell you that it was easy or fast at that time. It seemed painfully long with many lessons, setbacks and bumps along the way. I didn't have these tools then; nevertheless, every minute of the process was necessary for me and worth it. Healing does not have to take as long as many believe it does. You have the advantage of these tools given to you right here to help you heal much quicker and effectively. You will learn how to reprogram your mind in a way that God intended for it to speak to you. As a survivor of abandonment, childhood sexual abuse and child pornography, I was walking through this world feeling unlovable, unacceptable and unworthy of anything good. *Born to Bloom* helps to give you the truths of what God says about you. You will build and design your narration through this process and discover all the beautiful things God says about you! I learned the truth that I am loved, accepted and worthy of a life filled with peace from my past because of God's sacrifice for me, and for you too.

From the very first chapter, La Vonne will help you to understand God's love for you. You will not feel alone as you experience His presence knowing He is with you on this journey. This is going to give you the strength you need to grow and thrive. The truth is, we cannot be separated from the love of God no matter what transpires in our life. I now enjoy including God in everything I do, and I have found that as I ask for help during my most challenging days at work, during my interactions with others and during the smallest routine things, He gives me the confidence and power I need to succeed.

As you begin this life-changing process, this workbook will help you to explore your truths in each area and help you to fix your eyes on Jesus. Jesus knows what it is like to experience the pain people can inflict on us, and He knows the joy of coming out on the other side. You have within your hands the tools that will help you to become victorious and to completely heal! Together with God, La Vonne will help you to bloom and experience true joy and come out on the other side victoriously, truly healed with a sound mind that brings you peace. La Vonne will equip you to discover your purpose in helping others to heal as well. This is a beautiful journey that you will be grateful you took.

I am so grateful for La Vonne and the gift of friendship we share. I am thankful that she has developed this resource that will help you and so many others find the healing and hope they desire. It is being connected with godly people who understand what it means to walk the path of healing that I have been able to stay the course. I am praying for you, and excited to know that as you start this book, you will find the healing God has for you, and will have great hope for your bright future.

Carol Urton
Author, *When Hope Hurts*

Acknowledgments

I would like to thank my local rescue mission for allowing me the opportunity to develop this course and to trust me with the precious souls in need of healing. I would like to thank each and every person I worked with, for your patience, suggestions and edits while forming this program. Because of you many people will receive healing! Thank you! I am so grateful for my wonderful developmental editor, Michele Chiapetta, for helping me to compile all of my materials into a reader friendly workbook. I am grateful for Carla Green, who created the beautiful cover design and the internal formatting. I am grateful to my husband for supporting me and encouraging me to do the work that I do to help heal others. I am thankful for those of you who have gone through this course and offered your suggestions and reviews, you know who you are, and I appreciate you! Because of all of you, this workbook will help others realize their full potential and bloom into the person God created them to be.

How to Use This Book

Complete Healing from Any Form of Sexual Abuse is a seven-week interactive coaching course designed to help set men and women free from not only sexual abuse, but also any offense in your life. Through the concepts, tools, and activities in this book, you will learn how to develop a new and healthy inner narrator—a way of thinking based on healthy beliefs and biblical truths—to give you a sound mind and the happy life you deserve. **This workbook is intended to be used along with the seven-week video course found at www.YKIcoaching.com/borntobloom.**

Using the 5 Keys to Healing and Success

This book is built around a concept I use in my YKI coaching business—"The 5 Keys to Healing and Success" (which is also described in my book *A Coach for Christ*). Simply put, there are five steps we use as we move from a place where we are at, a place we wish to change, to a place where we are enjoying the fulfilled, happy, successful life we desire. These keys can be applied to any area of life and any issue we are facing.

In terms of healing from abuse, you'll use these keys over the next seven weeks to understand the effects of what you went through and begin to take practical steps toward the freedom God has for you. Here's what that will look like:

Key 1: Truth
God said you shall know the **truth,** and the **truth** will set you free (John 8:32). We examine truth in **Week 1**. Beginning with your spirituality, you'll ask yourself honestly what the truth is about the impact the abuse had on your life. Then, you'll move on to asking the same question for all the other areas of your life. This sets you up to begin to move from where you are right now to where you'd like to be.

Key 2: Goal
In **Week 2**, you will create a goal in each of the six key areas of your life that you will work on. Your goals will help you move toward healing, so you can accomplish the purposes God has for your life. For example, in the area of spirituality, you might decide to focus more on God's Word in your daily activities. Your **purpose** for each goal will drive it. For example, the purpose of meditating on God's Word is that it will bring healing and peace. making you more effective in all that you do.

Key 3: Plan

After you have set goals, you are ready to begin creating a **plan** for how you will accomplish your goals. It is much like deciding you will travel somewhere (the goal), and then writing down directions or highlighting the roads on a map (your plan) so you can begin to head toward your destination. In **Week 3**, you'll write down exactly what you are going to do to achieve each goal. For example, if your goal is to focus more on God's Word (the Bible), then your plan might be to get up 15 minutes early and spend those 15 minutes reading and meditating on a daily scripture.

Key 4: Action

In **Weeks 4, 5 and 6**, we'll look at the actions you can take to help you stick to your plans and accomplish your goals and purposes. You'll see how creating safe spaces, setting better boundaries, and connecting with safe, healthy people helps you stay on track toward success. You'll discover how choosing an accountability partner—someone of the same gender that you can trust—helps you keep moving toward your good and godly goals. Remember, it is important that you **follow through** with your plans for success. Without follow through, your goals are only dreams. Hold to your healing and success and make it happen!

Key 5: Success

Finally, in **Week 7**, we'll celebrate your accomplishments and see how continually following these 5 Keys will help you to enjoy a sound mind and a happy life. You will achieve **healing** and **success** when you hold close to God and follow these steps because He is faithful and will help you to follow through with your plans! Your **rewards** from the first four keys will begin to pour into your life. This is the point where the keys then must be repeated. And it is also the point when you can find ways to give back and bless others as you have been blessed.

As you enjoy the results of your healing, you can then begin to ask the questions, "What is the truth of why I have been blessed? What purpose can I move into, now that I am healed? Who will I help? What plan of action will I take to bless others?" Proverbs 11:25 in the Message translation tells us, *"The one who blesses others is abundantly blessed; those who help others are helped."* When we receive success and pass it on, it perpetuates our success.

Weekly Activities

Each section of this book includes an activities section to guide you daily on your road to healing. You'll find an encouraging, hope-filled scripture to think about and memorize daily, along with questions to guide you as you consider your life and take steps toward a bright future. There is space for writing in the book itself, or you can use a journal. The important thing is to do the daily activities so you can begin to move forward and find freedom.

There is also a section in each week's activities where you will write a "new narration" for yourself and have opportunities to add to that narration as you progress in your healing process. Your narration is a positive, faith-filled, encouraging, focused way to speak to yourself about who you are in Christ. As such, it is something you will highly personalize to reflect who God has created you to be, the truth about how He sees you and desires you to see yourself, along with your goals and purposes. There are examples in week one and in the Appendix to help you understand how to write your new narration and provide ideas that are helpful to you. Through your new narration, you will develop a new way of seeing and speaking to yourself, not as others have labeled you, not as a victim of abuse, but as a beloved child of God.

In addition to this book, videos and online groups are available to add to this course, check YKIcoaching.com for more details. This course is designed for group sessions, and there are safe group guidelines available for reference in the Appendix section. But you can also do the course alone and privately. (It is highly recommended that you have a safe, supportive person to talk to while doing this work. See disclaimer following this section for further information.)

Whether you are participating in a group or reading the book on your own, the process is similar. You will utilize each chapter's learning and tools for one week. During each week, there are daily activities, including a scripture to memorize and homework, usually in the form of questions to answer. You will work in one area per day, having one day off for rest each week.

As you do the work, prayerfully allow these coaching principles and methods to completely heal you from any form of abuse! This book gives you a place to safely share your story with yourself and God. If you are able to find safe people to share your story with as well, that's great! Support groups, counselors and Christian life coaches are all wonderful resources you may want to make use of as you heal. Always remember—God is faithful, and He will help you along the process to your healing and complete freedom.

Safe Group Guidelines

If you are using this book as part of a class or in a support group setting, it is essential to create a safe space for everyone to encourage each other, be open, and feel supported in a positive way. With that need in mind, here are some suggested guidelines for creating and maintaining a safe group:

1. Listen respectfully to everyone. — It is essential to create a space where people feel free to share their stories and receive validation.

2. Be patient with one another. — Our individual stories are complicated and challenging. At times, these stories may even feel exhausting to discuss.

3. Share as you feel comfortable doing so. — There should be no pressure for anyone to share when they are not ready to do so.

4. If sharing is causing discomfort for anyone in the group, it may be best to address the topic after the meeting privately.

5. Be accepting of the spiritual beliefs of others. — This book is focused on Christian principles, but in group settings there may be those who are not Christians. They may be of a different belief, a different religion, or may even be atheists. And this is okay. The purpose for the group is healing, and it is important to allow others to be themselves. As Christians, we believe everything that is good comes from God. As you encourage group members to move toward what is good, you will be helping them move toward what is godly.

6. Set up same-gender groups. — Sexual abuse is such an intimate subject! To create a sense of safety during discussions, facilitators should permit only people of the same gender into a group.

Disclaimer

This workbook and the methods contained herein are used at a local rescue mission where I volunteer and in private, one-on-one sessions in our office at YKI coaching. Because sexual abuse is so traumatic to the body, mind and spirit, the intended reader has had (or should take) ample time to seek medical attention and process the abuse immediately. This book's intention is to take the reader who is ready to process and move forward in their healing.

In no way is this book or the methods given within it meant to replace any needed medical or immediate mental attention. This book details the definition of sexual abuse in its many forms, along with the author's personal experiences toward helping one to heal from their personal trauma of any form of sexual abuse. The author is not a healthcare provider and does not offer medical opinions.

Except as specifically stated in this book, neither the author or publisher, nor any coauthors, editors, contributors, or other representatives of this book or YKI coaching will be liable for damages arising out of or in connection with the use of this book.

This is a comprehensive limitation of liability that applies to all damages of any kind. By using this book, you understand and agree that this book is not intended as a substitute for consultation with a licensed healthcare practitioner, such as your physician. Before you begin any healthcare program, or change your lifestyle in any way, you agree to consult your physician or another licensed healthcare practitioner to ensure that you are in good health and that the examples contained in this book will not harm you.

This book provides content related to physical and/or mental health issues. As such, use of this book implies your acceptance of this disclaimer.

YKI coaching's website, this book, and any related materials are an educational and consulting service that provides general leadership, communication, and change information. The materials in this book, and any materials from YKI coaching, are provided "as is" and without warranties of any kind either express or implied.

How to Use This Book

By reading this book, taking classes related to or using this book, or any of the seminars, workshops, and programs offered by YKI coaching, you are NOT engaging in a therapeutic relationship. If you need therapy, you are encouraged to engage the services of a mental health professional. Although La Vonne Earl is a master certified Christian coach, she is not offering therapy by providing the insights, suggestions and activities offered here, nor is she responsible for any mental health issues readers might have.

La Vonne Earl and the team at YKI coaching will support, assist, offer suggestions and encourage you, but are in no way responsible for your actions.

All decisions and actions are ultimately yours and yours alone to make.

Introduction

We all have things that impact us, but there are few things more impactful and hurtful than sexual abuse. It affects every area of one's life. To find healing, it is important to first gain an understanding of the truth of how sexual abuse has impacted one in their life. Abuse is defined as anything being used in a way it was unintended to be used. Sexual abuse is any area of sexuality being used in the way that God did *not* intend. This includes not only sexual intercourse but any sexual behaviors that violate what God intends—such as forcing someone to look at an inappropriate photo, forcing them to see nudity, and forcing someone to touch or be touched in an inappropriate way.

It is my desire to help the readers of this book to understand how the abuse they suffered has impacted their life so they can discover truth and make the changes necessary to gain the sound mind and happy life God intended for them to have! This is a journey I understand all too well. You see, I experienced sexual abuse as a young girl. And although my abuse might look different than yours, it impacted me in ways I didn't understand at the time, but those effects would later reveal why I would sabotage my own life in certain areas.

We cannot compare abuse; what may seem small or irrelevant to one may be extremely relevant and damaging to another. Any abuse, from mishandling sexual education all the way to actually harming one's body, has an impact! The principal concept to know is that abuse, whatever it may be, has an effect on us that we are wise to face so we can be healed.

My abuse happened when I was an 11-year-old girl. Although my mom claimed she had pure intentions to sexually educate my 13-year-old sister and me about what a man's body looks like, the situation she put us in caused great harm to my emotional health and the inward narration and beliefs I would develop, even unknowingly. This abusive decision my mother made would later cause an impact in my relationships and many other crucial areas of my life, such as emotional, physical and spiritual wellness. Because of the abuse, I felt I didn't have a voice in matters; it broke trust in my relationship with my mom, and also caused suspicion and mistrust in other relationships where trust should have been.

I didn't understand this for many years—until I developed the tools necessary to be set free! And I want to share what I learned to help you be free too.

Through using these tools, I have been able to understand truth in many areas and gain an understanding of what caused certain breakdowns. I have received my complete healing and am able to now operate with great success in my life! It is my goal and desire to see each and every woman and man receive their complete healing as well so that they can live the abundant life as intended! We can only live this happy life if we gain the sound mind this book will deliver.

Utilizing the methods I developed and this program that I teach to sex trafficked women, I have helped many victims gain an understanding of the impact from the abuse they endured, and taught them how to heal, how to set goals, develop their purpose and take the action steps necessary to achieve success. As you use this book, you will learn how to improve the six key areas of your life that have been impacted by the abuse. As I reveal them in this book, you will begin to assess the effects in your own life and take the transformative action steps to heal!

This book also reveals tools that will show you how to break free from the unhealthy beliefs that have developed in your life as a result of what you have experienced. You'll discover how you can reestablish a new, healthy inner narration—you know, that voice that speaks to you throughout your day, either knowingly or unknowingly. Your inner narration is based on the beliefs that you have developed from birth until now. We all develop beliefs based on the way people have attended to us, the environment that we have lived in, the things that have happened to us, our successes and failures. Many things are attributed to the narration we developed. You will learn how to intentionally develop the healthy narration needed to create and maintain a sound mind, so you can begin building the happy life that you deserve. You will learn how to apply these methods to not only heal from sexual abuse, but also how to coach yourself your entire life to keep your mind sound so you can live the abundant life intended for you!

Now, let's get started!

Week 1
You Are Not Alone

Be strong and courageous. Do not be afraid or terrified because of them,
for the Lord your God goes with you; he will never leave you nor forsake you.
— Deuteronomy 31:6 (NIV)

> *Suzette didn't know what to do or who to tell, but as a married woman she hated her life. She hated sex. She felt she didn't have a moment to herself and was frustrated each time she had to explain things to her children. Being a Christian, she prayed for patience, and to be able to give more love to her husband and children, but all she felt was hate. She felt like she was always giving, but not receiving in return. This caused her to feel guilt and regret, and to wish she were never born. At times, she thought about ending it all. Each morning, she opened her eyes hoping something would change, but she had no idea where to even begin.*

Does this story sound at all familiar? Perhaps you feel similarly or have felt this way at times in your life. Maybe you can relate to what Suzette is going through. If you are reading this book, then you have likely found yourself feeling that in some way, you'd like your life to be different, yet you don't know how to make the changes needed. Perhaps you have even prayed to God for help, but it seems as if He has not answered.

If so—if this is speaking to you—then I want you to know that this book will have answers for you. I want you to know that you are incredibly brave simply for being here and choosing to pursue healing from the hurts and pains of your past. And this book is going to help you not only to receive healing, but also it will equip you to stay strong and healthy. The tools here will be of such great benefit to you for the rest of your life, and I am excited to take this journey with you so you can experience all the goodness that God has planned for you!

Let's begin!

The Power of Loving and Being Loved by God

"Even if the mountains were to crumble and the hills disappear,
my heart of steadfast, faithful love will never leave you,
and my covenant of peace with you will never be shaken,"
says Yahweh,
whose love and compassion will never give up on you.
— Isaiah 54:10 (TPT)

First and foremost, you need to know **you are loved!** If your only takeaway from this book is that you are deeply, completely loved by God, we will have succeeded in giving you a new way of seeing yourself that can transform the rest of your life. You are worthy of His love, because He chose to love you. First John 3:1 (NIV) says it this way: *See what great love the Father has lavished on us, that we should be called children of God! And that is what we are!*

You didn't have to do anything to earn His love. And you don't have to prove yourself to Him now. You are worthy of being loved, because you are His child, and *God is love!* He sees you through loving eyes, and He wants you to know how valuable and beloved you truly are.

For some of you, the very idea that you are loved and are worthy of being loved is a new concept. You have felt betrayed, taken advantage of and abused, and I am so very sorry you have gone through this. You have made it through some very tough situations. Now, through the tools you will learn in this book, God is going to heal you and restore you!

Though it may be hard to imagine living a life of healing, restoration and joy, it is something God can help you achieve. The message of hope and beauty is all around us, written into the creation He made for us to enjoy. Yes, God has made many beautiful things on this earth to give us encouragement if we will look for them.

One of my favorite examples of God's faithful ability to create something amazing from even the darkest places is the lotus flower. The lotus plant has a flower which was designed to bloom. Its journey begins in the deep mud found at the bottom of ponds and rivers, which means it doesn't get to receive the sun for growth when it is first digging its roots into the earth. But because the lotus plant is so determined to bloom, it fights its way through the water, rises above the muck, and blossoms into a beautiful flower!

By being here, reading this book, and committing yourself to being free of the abuse you endured, you are just like this beautiful, white lotus flower. You are strong. You're courageous. You are so loved by God! And you are going to have a new beginning filled with purity and other beautiful qualities that God is bestowing on you as you make your journey to healing!

Here is another thing to realize about being loved. Those who know they are loved make good choices that enable them to take care of themselves. They do so because they know they are valued and important, and so they treat themselves that way. It's like owning a precious diamond. If you owned a jewel that was unique, beautiful, and had tremendous worth, you wouldn't simply toss it away or leave it somewhere that it could get lost or damaged. You would put it somewhere safe, somewhere it could be protected from any harm. You would treasure and value it because you know how much it is worth.

You are that precious jewel! You are of tremendous value to God, so valuable that He sent His Son Jesus for your sake. He loves you more than anyone can measure. As you come to love yourself and know your own worth, you will find it easier to do the things that keep you safe, healthy, and well.

Each day, and every moment of the day, I encourage you to draw upon this truth that God loves you. Try to bring your awareness to God's love for you into all that you do. Trust in Him, because He can provide the right people in your life to restore you and help bring healing. Be patient with the process and with yourself, and lean into Jesus and His safe, protecting, guiding love for you.

I want you to know this as well: God will be with you constantly! That's His own promise to you in Deuteronomy 31:8. He never leaves you! You are never alone. When you need prayer, He is there. When you need comfort, He is there. Whatever your needs are, turn your thoughts to Jesus and ask Him! He will answer, and He will be there!

Your Story and God's Story

So faith comes from hearing, and hearing through the word of Christ.
— **Romans 10:17 (ESV)**

All stories have a beginning, a middle and an end. This concept will be one key to your path to healing. Let me explain.

Your own personal story is very important, of course. We all have our own lives filled with events that make up our personal stories. The situations you have endured, the abuse you have gone through, is a part of that story. It may be so much in your mind that it seems to be all you can think about. Or you may try to push the memories out of your mind, yet the past creeps into the way you live your life, causing you to act from a place of woundedness instead of well-being.

You are going to gain so much power as you begin to recognize how your personal story has affected you. After all, knowledge is powerful. It can also be transformative as you use that knowledge to shape your decisions. As you think of your story, remember that there is much to be written in this life and through eternity. What you experienced is one part of your life, but it is not the end. There is so much more to your present and future.

It is also important to look beyond yourself to see the bigger story for your life—the purpose that God desires for you to fulfill. There is a beginning to your life which you have already lived. There is a middle, which is where you are at right now and where you are heading. And there is a beautiful "end," which really begins your future and eternity in heaven with God.

Often, when we are going through horrible and hard times, the middle part of our story— the now—feels overwhelming. We can't see past it. We may lose hope. And this is where I want to encourage you that there is hope for a good and godly future that brings you joy and success! As you begin to heal from past abuse, you will gain a sound mind and well-being, and you will experience the happy life God intended for you! You have a beautiful life ahead of you!

It all starts with healing, which begins as you take a look at yourself and consider the areas of your life where the woundedness from your past is having an impact. We will do that later in this chapter. But your healing also comes when you begin to see that there is a purpose that can grow out of your past pain. It comes as you begin to see that the abuse you went through is not the end for you. It is only one part of a much larger story that God wants you to play a role in.

Yes, God also has a Story, one that is so much bigger than a single human being, and yet we are each so important in it because He loves us so much. The Big God Story begins long before you and I were ever born, when the world and human beings were first created. His Story has continued for thousands of years as He worked in the lives of human beings like Adam and Eve, Abraham, Noah, Ruth, Esther, and so many others. He sent His own Son, Jesus, to give His life for our sins on the cross, to redeem us. And He is present here right now, to be with you in your life, and to work through you to bring about good, not just for you but for those you can help too.

You have an important part to play in the Big God Story! What the enemy intended to use to hurt you, God is going to use to bring about good. He will heal you and allow your pain to be used for the greatest purpose of all, which is to help many people heal! Right now, that might feel overwhelming. You might wonder how you could possibly help others. But once you become healed, I promise you that you will be so filled with joy, it will be hard to contain!

As you use this book to discover the impact your past has had on your life, you will begin to move toward a new purpose for your life. God will heal you, and He will use you to bless others. God will make your life better than you could have ever imagined!

Understanding Sexual Abuse

I trust in God's unfailing love for ever and ever.
— Psalm 52:8 (NIV)

Abuse, by its very definition, is the improper use of something. In other words, abuse is using something in a way it was *not* intended or designed to be used. When applied to people, sexual abuse occurs when someone uses you or forcefully exposes themselves to you in a way that God did not intend.

You may really know and understand that you were abused. Or, you may still be confused about what happened. You might feel that since your experience wasn't against your will and you willingly got into something that led to abuse, you were not abused. Or maybe you were too young to put things into words. Maybe you loved your abuser and so desired to please him or her, but you were underage and ill prepared to make such a decision. Maybe you buried it for many years, and you forgot until you had something trigger you to remember.

Or maybe you were like me, confused for many years until one day when Pastor Rick Warren gave the definition of sexual abuse, and it clarified the impact I had experienced as an 11-year-old girl. The definition he gave that day at church was this: abuse is any visual, verbal or physical activity that occurs without your consent.

Everyone has a different story and a different experience; no pain is too great or too small to God. To help you gain clarity on your situation, simply ask yourself if the act you experienced was the way God intended sexual intimacy to be and you will have your answer, and you will be ready to move forward with your healing.

What is proper sexual intimacy as God intends it to be?

First of all, intimacy means "into me see," and it is a level of sharing who we are with others. It does not always include sex. For example, to be intimate between friends is to share parts of our life so we can each get to know one another better. No sex is involved at all. We can have appropriate intimate conversations with our children where we share things with them in a safe, godly fashion. And of course, no sex is involved.

The only intimacy involving sex that God intends for there to be is that which occurs lovingly between a husband and wife. This form of intimacy involves more than the act of sex. It is protective and safe. It feels good and doesn't hurt. And it is within God's will, not outside of His will.

So, as you consider what you experienced in the past, or even may be experiencing now, you can consider whether the intimacy you've had has been safe, honest, protective, healthy sharing, or if it has not. You can also ask yourself if you were taught or brought up in a way that would lead you to true sexual intimacy. If you weren't taught this when you were younger, this can help to explain what has caused you to make some of the choices that you did. You simply didn't know what God desired for you, because it was not properly taught to you.

Whatever the case may be, know this: God loves you. He desires to heal you and to restore you in every area! Learn from God's way of interacting with people. He is safe. He is true love and true intimacy! He desires to be close to you, to protect you, to cleanse your mind and to give you peace. His true intimacy sees every part of your life and your heart, and He loves you. Learn true intimacy with Him alone, and you will be completely healed! He will restore you!

Abuse Comes in Many Forms

As mentioned already above, people often mistakenly believe that sexual abuse, including childhood sexual abuse, is limited to just a specific physical act, but many forms of sexual abuse exist. Forced exposure, forced touching, and anything inappropriate regarding our privacy and our minds are considered abuse and definitely not the way God intended intimacy. This is worth repeating: If the act made you feel ashamed, if it felt wrong or hurtful, if you said no and were not heard, then it was inappropriate in some way.

If you are still uncertain, the Bible does a beautiful job of defining for us appropriate behavior in verses such as Galatians 5:22–23, which tells us the fruit of God's Holy Spirit is love, joy, peace, forbearance, kindness, goodness, faithfulness, gentleness and self-control. This shows us how God intends for us to treat one another. And it is also how God treats us.

God hates abuse in any form! His design and desires are for us to enjoy protection, safety, care, love, and concern from those we are intimate with, including Him! God is the perfect example of love in that He lays down His life for us. *Love doesn't hurt others. So loving is the same as obeying all the law* (Romans 13:10 ERV).

Sometimes sexual abuse can be confusing because it is not always physically painful, or it is entwined with our feelings of love for the person who abused us. It becomes even more confusing when the abuse was performed by a family member, or someone you were very close to prior to the abuse. Those who should have protected you and helped teach you God's design for intimacy instead took advantage of you.

Many times, people fall prey to the wrong people in their life, the people who can hurt them, because they are vulnerable. They are seeking love and can choose unsafe people to try to get the love they crave. Often, they may have suffered childhood emotional neglect (CEN), and because of it they are seeking love from the wrong people. When very young children are abused by someone within the family or close to the family, they often protect the abuser because they love them and are still seeking to be loved. This is never the child's fault.

But as we grow into adulthood, we have more options available to us, more opportunities to take control of our lives. Seeking love from unhealthy people, however, will keep one stuck. Through this book, God and I will help you to develop your inner strength so that you can stand for truth and accept only true love from safe people.

Sex is only to be had between a husband and wife where love and healthy intimacy are present. Sexual abuse, by contrast, does not involve love or intimacy! The sexual abuse you experienced was done by twisted minds who did not love God or seek to protect anyone! Abusive people are not thinking in ways that are healthy and godly. They have misguided or wrong intentions, and as a result, take wrong actions that create harm. The abuse was a misuse of someone's power and strength as they sought to control you. It was against God's true design for you.

Those days are over! You are now operating in your strength, power and control, as God intends! Just reading this book demonstrates that you are strong and courageous!

Let's learn more so you can heal that wound!

The Impact of Sexual Abuse

Surely God is my help; the Lord is the one who sustains me.
— **Psalm 54:4 (NIV)**

The trauma of sexual abuse has a profound impact on every area of our lives. It can lead us into ways of thinking that are not good and godly. We can find ourselves believing things about ourselves and others that are not based in truth. It is hard to have a happy life filled with peace and purpose if we don't have a sound mind. This is how we can find ourselves stuck in cycles of failure and discouragement.

On the other hand, healing comes as we learn to separate the lies and negative thoughts from God's truth. As we face what happened and assess how it has impacted us, we can begin to make decisions that allow change, growth and increasing freedom. As we heal, we can begin to have success and live a life that we truly enjoy.

As you go through your story using the daily healing exercises in this chapter, you will discover the effects that abuse has had on you. As John 8:32 says, you will know the truth, and the truth will set you free! Knowing truth through these activities will help you throughout your life, as you continue to grow as a disciple of Jesus Christ. With the skills you gain now, you will learn how to coach yourself throughout your life, setting yourself up to obtain your good and godly goals. You will develop a new inner narrator that speaks to you the way God would speak to you!

In this way, God will heal you and empower you to live fully the wonderful, beautiful, joyful life He intends for you to enjoy.

Discovering the Effects of Your Past in the Six Key Areas of Life

As you begin to evaluate where you are at in life right now, it is helpful to understand that your life is made up of six key areas: spirituality, relationships, emotional health, physical health, finances, and career, which includes serving others. It can be helpful to use this image of a circle as a picture of this. The center of the circle is Christ. Our lives will be richly blessed as we allow Him to be our center and focus, helping us in each area of our life.

In an ideal world such as heaven, each of these areas is meant to be rich, full, healthy, and balanced. In reality, we all find ourselves sometimes out of balance or in need of growth in one or more areas of our life. What is most important for you to understand right now is that each of these areas affects the others. When one area of our life is out of balance in some way, it spills into other areas too. It is helpful for us to assess each area and to recognize where we are at right now, so that we can see opportunities to heal and grow.

I want to share a part of my own story of abuse as an example of how the impact can spill over into other areas of our lives. These effects can impact us in ways we may not even recognize until we look closely at them and understand the truth.

When I was a young girl of 11 years old, I was playing with my Barbie dolls. My sister, who was 13, was also in our room. Suddenly, my mom came in, having decided that this would be the day she would teach my sister and me about a man's penis and sex. She took us into her dark room where my stepdad was lying in bed naked.

Though I was too young to understand exactly what was happening, I could definitely sense that something was very wrong with the situation. We all know intuitively that everyone's private parts are to remain private. I began to cry and told my mom I wanted to leave. Instead of listening to me and respecting what I was asking for, my mom insisted that I kneel down next to the bed. Then she forced me to touch my stepdad's penis so she could "teach" my sister and me about it.

I was greatly disturbed by this event. And although nothing more happened that day, this one abusive act impacted my life greatly.

It impacted my **emotional** life because I always felt like something was wrong with me, that somehow, I was different and didn't fit in. It affected my **identity** because I felt I didn't have a voice and that no one listened to me. When someone forces you to do something, this often happens. It affected me **spiritually** as I would wrongly believe that God was a controlling God and that I couldn't trust Him. It affected me **relationally** as I took this baggage into my married life, not knowing I needed to be healed. Many of the wrong beliefs I developed would spill into other areas, causing me to make poor choices and causing me to be vulnerable to other abuse.

Understanding How Abusive People Think

The interesting thing about abusive people is that they are obviously not thinking or acting correctly. They make choices based on the wrong beliefs or intentions, which leads them to take wrong actions. Therefore, the rest of their life is usually as messy as their abusive actions. Their faulty thinking, decisions and behaviors spill into every area of their lives, leading to further problems.

This was true for my mom, as she was a neglectful mother in certain areas, causing me to suffer from Childhood Emotional Neglect (CEN) as well. I grew up feeling unloved and not wanted in addition to other negative beliefs about myself. My mom was married four times with other children from her fourth husband. They often participated in activities that I was not included in, causing me to develop additional negative beliefs such as "I am not wanted and not a part of a family." I had to "unlearn" and recover from my faulty "narration" in order to be free as God intends me to be.

Parents and guardians who are neglectful increase the likelihood that one will be abused in the future. When you are neglected, as I was, you tend to hang around the wrong people, looking for love. The problem is they cannot offer true love to anyone because they are not safe people to be around. These people are abusive in many forms, causing the cycle of abuse to continue until we take the steps needed to break the chains of dysfunction and abuse and find healing.

This is why I tell you that this book is going to show you how to coach yourself from any area of abuse and dysfunction. I was impacted in each of the six key areas of life, and I needed to be set free in order to have the sound mind I have and live the abundant life I do now. And what I've learned, I'm sharing with you. This workbook will serve as your guide and help you gain the strategies you need to achieve a sound mind and happy life as well!

A Prayer for You

Dear Lord, I am lifting my friend going through this book up to You. I pray that as they process the hurt from their abuse, they will feel Your presence with them continually. I ask that they know and feel that they are loved, safe and secure. I pray You give them wisdom and new revelations that help them to live an intentional and purpose-filled life! Help them to see the big picture of their life and the grander picture of their future! Help them to have great vision for all the great plans that You have for them! Give them a new narrator that speaks to them the way You would. In Jesus' name, amen.

DAILY HEALING ACTIVITIES

God came to give you life (John 10:10)! His desire for you is that you do not fear, that instead you live in peace! As you focus on Him and His Word, your mind will be transformed into one of peace, calm, contentment, and power. As you live in His Holy Spirit and Word, you will focus on that which is good and pleasing.

To aid you in this process, I have included daily exercises for you to do, including both scriptures to learn and questions to answer. There is a scripture listed with each day's activities. Take that scripture and memorize it. Let it be your mantra that day—what you say over and over again until it is firmly planted in your mind and has sunk deeply into your heart. Meditate on the scripture. Visualize it with every detail that you can, details that include you, your name, and yourself experiencing what the scripture means.

In addition, begin to explore the impact of your past by answering the suggested questions each day. Let the questions listed here act as a guide to aid you as you seek to become more aware of where you are at right now. Go through the daily questions to help you discover what has happened in your life and how abuse impacted these areas. Work on one area at a time, ideally one area each day.

I encourage you to find one safe person to process the questions with and allow them to support you and encourage you. The accountability and support partner you choose should be of the same gender as you, and they can be either from the group you are studying this book with or from your personal life. They should be someone you trust—a person who is healthy in their thinking and behavior, one who respects you and has proper boundaries.

Also, spend time on this alone, asking God to show you what impact the abuse had in each area. Invite Him to speak to your heart and allow Him to comfort you and love you as you take the brave steps toward seeking the healing and freedom you deserve!

Week 1: You Are Not Alone

Day 1: Spirituality

Memorize this scripture:

Do not yield to fear, for I am always near. Never turn your gaze from me, for I am your faithful God. I will infuse you with my strength and help you.
— Isaiah 41:10 (TPT)

Use these questions to guide you as you explore your past's impact on your spiritual life. Remember that you are discovering the impact, which is often negative, but as you do so, you are also going to be building the areas in your life that are lacking or in need with the positive, life building words from God that He desires for you.

After you go through the questions, take any negative word and replace it with a positive word and add it to your narration.

For a reminder of what a godly narration does, see the Weekly Activities description in the section on How to Use This Book. Refer also to the description of writing your narration that appears at the end of this chapter, as well as the sample godly narrations in the Appendix.)

(Here are some examples of spiritual impact to help you get started: not trusting God, feeling that God failed to protect you, your sense of spirituality is twisted or harmful in some way, etc.)

1. How did the abuse impact you spiritually?

2. What is your relationship like with God?

3. Do you trust Him?

4. Where do you think He was during your abuse?

5. Do you think your abuse hurt His heart?

6. How do you feel about God?

7. What kind of relationship do you have with Him?

8. What kind of relationship do you want with Him?

9. Is it easy or hard for you to talk with the Lord about your abuse?

10. What one word or more did the abuse remove from you spiritually? Examples: trust, loved, etc. (Write these positive words in your godly narration at the end of this chapter.)

11. Do you believe God desires to heal you?

12. Do you believe He is powerful enough to heal you?

13. Do you believe God saved you? In what ways?

14. What do you want your future to be like?

15. What steps can you take to get there?

Day 2: Relationships

Memorize this scripture:

Do not be anxious about anything, but in every situation, by prayer and petition, with thanksgiving, present your requests to God. And the peace of God, which transcends all understanding, will guard your hearts and your minds in Christ Jesus.
— Philippians 4:6 (NIV)

Use these questions to guide you as you explore your past's impact on your relationships.

(Here are some examples of relationship impact to help you get started: you didn't feel heard, didn't have a voice, found it hard to form healthy relationships, etc.)

1. How did the abuse affect your previous relationships?

2. How does it affect your current relationships?

3. Is the impact from your abuse keeping you from relationships you would like to have?

4. Does anyone particular stand out to you who is causing you grief?

Week 1: You Are Not Alone

5. Is there anyone you need to forgive?

6. What one word or more would you use to describe any difficulty you have in relationships? Examples include broken trust, unforgiveness, etc. (Write these positive words in your godly narration at the end of this chapter. Examples: trusting, forgiving)

7. Do you have relationships that drain you?

8. Do you fellowship with—meaning, hang out with, go to church with, do life with—other believers?

9. Do you have safe people in your life that you can talk to? Tell your story to?

10. How would you like to improve your relationships?

11. What steps do you need to take to improve them?

12. Do you have supportive relationships?

13. Who do you turn to for prayer? Encouragement?

14. Who can you encourage?

15. What type of relationships would you like to have?

Week 1: You Are Not Alone

Day 3: Emotional Health

Memorize this scripture:

When I am afraid, I put my trust in You.
— Psalm 56:3 (NIV)

Use these questions to guide you as you explore your past's impact on your emotional health.

(Here are some examples of emotional impact to help you get started: feeling insecure, lacking a sense of confidence, feeling like you don't make a difference, etc.)

1. What kind of impact did the abuse have on your emotions?

   _____
   _____
   _____

2. What one word or words describe you emotionally?

   _____
   _____
   _____

3. How would you like to be described? (Write these positive words in your godly narration at the end of this chapter.)

   _____
   _____
   _____

4. Do you believe you can completely heal?

   _____
   _____
   _____

5. In what ways have you allowed abuse to define who you are?

6. Do you believe you are victorious? Strong?

7. What one word or words were taken from you emotionally because of the abuse? (Write these positive words in your godly narration at the end of this chapter.)

8. Would you like those words and feelings to be restored?

9. Do you believe these words and feelings can be restored?

10. What would you like your new identity to become?

Day 4: Physical Health

Memorize this scripture:

Beloved friend, I pray that you are prospering in every way and that you continually enjoy good health, just as your soul is prospering.
— 3 John 1:2 TPT

Use these questions to guide you as you explore your past's impact on your physical health.

(Here are some examples of physical impact to help you get started: gaining weight as a way to protect yourself, finding comfort in food, reluctance to appear attractive, fear of being enticing, not caring for one's well-being, etc.)

1. What impact did the abuse have on you physically?

2. Have you done anything physically to alter yourself because of the abuse?

3. What did you come to believe about yourself physically because of the abuse?

4. What would you like to believe about yourself physically? (Write these positive words in your godly narration at the end of this chapter.)

5. Are there any ways that you would like to change physically?

6. Do you enjoy exercise?

7. Do you have any routines to keep your physical health in good shape?

8. How has the impact of abuse affected your health?

9. Do you consider yourself healthy?

10. Do you believe you can live a healthy life?

Week 1: You Are Not Alone

11. Are there any ways that you are allowing ill health because of the abuse?

   _____

   _____

   _____

12. What health goals would you like to achieve?

   _____

   _____

   _____

Day 5: Financial Health

Memorize this scripture:

And my God will supply every need of yours according to his riches in glory in Christ Jesus.
— Philippians 4:19 (ESV)

Use these questions to guide you as you explore your past's impact on your financial health.

(Here are some examples of financial impact to help you get started: not feeling capable of handling money or bills, not feeling deserving of abundance, feeling powerless when it comes to finances, overspending or underspending, not managing money effectively, etc.)

1. How has the abuse affected you financially?

   _____
   _____
   _____

2. Is there anything you believe about finances because of the abuse?

   _____
   _____
   _____

3. What would you like to believe about money? (Write these positive words in your godly narration at the end of this chapter.)

   _____
   _____
   _____

4. What financial goals would you like to achieve?

   _____
   _____
   _____

5. Do you believe you can achieve them?

6. How would your life be different once you achieve these financial goals?

7. What one word or words describe how you feel about money? (Write these positive words in your godly narration at the end of this chapter.)

8. What will you do with your money once you achieve that success?

9. In what ways can you bless others without money? With money?

10. Do you feel you need to learn more about finances so you can handle them better?

Day 6: Career and Serving Others

Memorize this scripture:

O Lord our God, let your sweet beauty rest upon us and give us favor. Come work with us, and then our works will endure, and give us success in all we do.
— Psalm 90:17 TPT

Use these questions to guide you as you explore your past's impact on your career and ministry.

(Here are some examples of career and serving impact to help you get started: feeling like you have no choice in what you can do or be, feeling there are no resources available to help you succeed, a sense that you won't have what it takes to be a success, etc. Write these positive words in your godly narration at the end of this chapter.)

1. In what way has the abuse affected your career?

2. Do you believe you have career choices?

3. How has abuse affected the way you help others?

4. Has the abuse limited any beliefs about what you can do professionally?

Week 1: You Are Not Alone

5. If you could do anything, what would you do?

6. What do you feel your strengths and talents are?

7. What are you passionate about?

8. Do you feel obligated or pressured?

9. How do you feel about serving the Lord?

10. Are you able to brighten or bless someone through your work? Outside of work?

11. What is your career or ministry goals?

_____
_____
_____

Day 7: Sabbath Rest

Memorize this scripture:

Are you weary, carrying a heavy burden? Then come to me. I will refresh your life, for I am your oasis. Simply join your life with mine. Learn my ways and you'll discover that I'm gentle, humble, easy to please. You will find refreshment and rest in me.
— Matthew 11:28-29 TPT

Do something to relax and restore yourself today!

Today, there are no questions to answer. Instead, take this day of rest to enjoy yourself and love yourself. Show yourself some care. Here are some suggestions, and you can choose the one that appeals to you or come up with something equally relaxing and restorative:

- Read your godly narration from this week to encourage yourself. (Suggestion: read it twice a day, morning and night. If you need help creating your godly narration, look at the "How to Use This Book" and "Appendix" sections in this book for guidance and ideas.)

- Take a walk in a beautiful park or on the beach, enjoying nature.

- Watch a funny, light-hearted movie that makes you laugh and smile.

- Play with your pet. Be affectionate and enjoy their affection toward you.

- Make a healthy meal that you like the taste of and that helps you feel good about yourself.

- Call someone who is a good friend and catch up on each other's days.

- Grab your favorite drink (tea, lemonade, or something similar) and relax on your porch, listening to the sounds of life around you.

Write Your Inner Narration

Each of us has an inner narrator—a voice inside our heads that reflects how we think about ourselves and how we talk to ourselves.

As a result of the abuse you experienced, your inner voice can become negative, saying things to you that are hurtful or judgmental. You may tell yourself things that an abusive person said to you, such as, "You are ugly" or "You are unwanted." Or you may tell yourself things that place the blame for the abuse on you, such as, "You are a bad person" or "You deserve for people to hurt you." But these are not things God would say to you. This is not how He speaks to His beloved children—you and me!

Remember that God's words are positive. His words lift and encourage you. What He says is the exact opposite of the negative thoughts and lies that you have been led to believe due to abuse. In the Appendix, there is a list of common lies people tend to believe about themselves, as well as the positive, loving, real things God says are true about us. Looking at this list to see what you have believed about yourself and comparing it to who God says you are in Him is one way to discover who He has truly made you to be — a beautiful, well-loved, valuable person who is pleasing to Him because you are His child.

Faith comes by what we hear. *So faith comes from hearing, that is, hearing the Good News about Christ* (Romans 10:17 NLT). The problem is, you have heard the wrong message in your life, perhaps from those you once trusted the most. Knowing the truth is the first step you take to leaving the lies that hurt you behind. As you get His words, His truth, deep into your innermost being, your heart, then His words can turn into reality in your life.

We do this with an activity that I call "writing your inner narration." To do this activity, think about some of the negative lies and words you have learned to think and speak about yourself. Some of these words will be in the answers to the questions for this week. Look up these words in the Appendix and find positive, faith-filled, godly words that are the opposite, and start writing something out that describes how you would like to see yourself, and what God has to say about who you are.

Here is an example of a godly, encouraging, positive narration to get you started:

I am beautiful. I am loved by God, just as I am. I am forgiven. I am pleasing to God.
I am strong. I am courageous…

Follow that pattern and additionally write something else below that fits with how God sees you and how you want to see yourself. Then read and say this narration out loud at least twice a day, morning and night. Read it over and over, especially when you are feeling discouraged. Speak it over yourself like a prayer every chance you get. It will begin to get into your heart and mind, and with each day, it will feel more and more natural to think about yourself with an inner narration that is lined up with God's truth — which is the real you!

Your Inner Narration

I am beautiful. I am loved by God, just as I am. I am forgiven. I am pleasing to God. I am strong. I am courageous…

Week 2
Choosing to Heal

We must let go of every wound that has pierced us and the sin we so easily fall into.
— Hebrews 12:1 (TPT)

> *Bridgette slapped her child and then proceeded to spank her until her little 6-year-old bottom was red. Her daughter had simply not gone to her room when she asked, yet the disrespect was more than Bridgette could take. As her daughter lay in her room crying, Bridgette sat on the couch and began to cry too. She felt guilt, anger, resentment. She felt alone and incapable. How could she admit that she was an abusive mother? She felt it deep within her and she knew she needed help, yet would she lose her daughter? Would her husband think she was a failure, and possibly divorce her? Her secrets were killing her.*

One result of abuse that many people face is feelings like Bridgette describes above. Fears, despair, vulnerability, and shame can all arise, causing us to feel that we are failures—that we are displeasing even to God. Choosing to "let go of the wounds" and choosing to heal will help us move forward and be set free of the feelings of guilt and pain that arise from the past abuse we experienced.

I want to encourage you that as a victim of sexual abuse, in no way does the word *sin* in Hebrews 12:1 indicate you. You were wounded. You were sinned against. Sin is against God's design of what His best is for you. God did not want this abuse to happen to you. It was not part of His plan. His plans are good! *"For I know the plans I have for you,"* declares the Lord, *"plans to prosper you and not to harm you, plans to give you hope and a future"* (Jeremiah 29:11 NIV).

Even though someone else sinned against you, you are still dealing with the effects of what that person did to you. This means you need to heal the wound and let go of it so you can be whole, transformed, and not act out from a place of being wounded. When we act out of the wounded place, we end up wounding others, which then becomes our sin.

Bridgette's situation is an example of this. In dealing with her daughter in an abusive way, she was acting from a place of being wounded. Although she may not have understood it at the moment, she lost control; the abuse from her past was being repeated in the form of abuse toward her daughter. Bridgette is only one example of the many ways we can sin because we are hurt. After all, hurt people hurt others. We don't want to become abusers ourselves so it is very important to get the help that we need so we can break the chains of abuse.

Knowing Our Triggers

These mad outrages that a victim experiences are caused because they are being triggered, which means a wound has been touched. I also like to call these triggers "fake buttons." You may have heard the phrase, "they are pushing my buttons." Buttons or triggers occur mostly when we are unaware of what is happening within us. We become enraged and we usually do not understand why. This is why God has said, *"You will know the truth, and the truth will set you free"* (John 8:32 NLT). (We will discuss triggers in more detail in Week 5.)

Bridgette had a fake button telling her that she was being disrespected. When that false belief felt like it was being pushed, it caused her to feel wounded again, just as she was wounded by the abuse in her past. The feeling of hurt therefore led her to completely overact with her daughter. Had she done the work of discovering the impact of abuse on her life, she would have discovered that she felt greatly disrespected by what happened to her during the act of abuse. Perhaps in addition to the act itself, she was slapped. She acted out with her daughter in an angry, self-protecting way because of the abuse she experienced. But the act was misplaced, because her daughter wasn't the source of the wound.

This is why I refer to the tools in this book as being helpful to heal more than sexual abuse. There are abusive and neglectful acts we can suffer from that are not sexual, yet they cause us to feel disrespected, unloved, disregarded and so much more! When we learn and understand how we truly felt and were impacted by our past, we can then begin the work of not only healing the wound but also changing our inner narration, so that we see ourselves as God sees us and know and feel respected, loved, cherished and more!

Appreciate Your Value

So, are you ready to be healed? To act from a place of victory? Once we are healed, we can help others instead of wounding them. Go ahead and add the words *respected, valued* and *loved* to your narration. This is how you are to think, feel and talk about yourself because you are respected, valued and loved! And so much more!

Understanding your value is going to position you in a place of victory, so that you no longer sabotage your life. Imagine healed Bridgette feeling loved, respected and valued. She is then going to speak to her daughter in a way that shows that she loves, respects and values her daughter. When her daughter refuses to go to her room, she might calmly and gently say something like, "Honey, I know that you love and respect mommy, as I love and respect you. I am asking you to please go to your room. If you refuse, you are going to lose the privilege of staying up until 8 p.m. and will have to go to bed right after dinner. I love you. I hope you will choose wisely."

Can you see what a difference that approach would make? It would help Bridgette feel in control of her response and proud of herself. It would encourage her daughter and feel loving. Both mother and daughter would be able to interact in a healthy way, which allows for more closeness and greater joy!

The Glory of Being Healed

Behold, I will bring to it health and healing, and I will heal them
and reveal to them abundance of prosperity and security.
— Jeremiah 33:6 (ESV)

When you are healed of your inner woundedness, you can accomplish so much more and you will gain even more respect for yourself and others, bringing more and more blessings into your life! Healing is God's provision in this broken world! God wants you healed. God provided our healer in Jesus! Jesus came to remove all sin, by becoming sin for us. He came to die in our place so that we could become the righteousness of God (2 Corinthians 5:21). That means if we become the righteousness of God, we become pure and holy as He is! Wow!

Everything that Jesus is, we become when we accept Him into our heart! We will never be perfect in this life, but we are perfected because of Jesus! Little by little even here in the flesh, when we seek Him and His love that heals, we begin to look and act more like Him each day.

I Choose to Heal

Choosing to heal is really about your choice. God desires to heal you! He wants to go through the entire process of finding healing, restoration, freedom and joy with you! It is a process, and you will need to face it and walk through it, but remember you are never alone! God is with you through it all.

Choosing to heal means you are willing to:

1. Face the truth.
Facing the truth of what happened is a very courageous step. Many people walk in denial throughout their life, postponing the healing that is available in truth and awareness. You know the abuse occurred. Through your work in week 1 of this book, you have explored the six key areas of your life to discover the truth of where you are at in your life right now. And you will continually be unveiling how the abuse and other things in your life impacted each area.

2. Change and heal.

This self-examination is a lifelong process for all of us, even if a person hasn't been sexually abused. Different events in our life impact us all, and the more we are aware of what is happening and how it is impacting us, the more we will learn, heal and grow in a positive way!

Are you willing to change the way you think and deal with things? Are you ready to heal? I know that this concept may sound scary to you. But I believe in you! I know you are courageous because you are reading this book right now and you want to make the changes necessary to gain a sound mind and a happy life! We are doing this together! Let's make the plans you need to do so!

3. Plan for success

It is important to plan for the success you desire, no matter what that success is! Healing is your first goal and why you are here. You are going to plan for your success using the tools you are learning in this book.

4. Be held accountable.

Allowing other safe people to speak into your life is very important. We all need to be held accountable by others. The more you allow a safe person (someone who is healthy, respectful and has proper, godly boundaries) to hold you accountable for the way you think and act, the quicker you will heal.

It is important for this safe person to listen to what you are going through, and to help you process (think through and discover things about) your story. This person should not force you to share. This is your story and you get to tell as much or as little as you desire. Your safe person is someone who can help you to focus on your future, and the Big God Story, to help get the focus off of yourself, after you have processed what happened to you.

5. Help others.

As you are walking out your healing process, it is also valuable and helpful to think of the purpose of your pain and how you can serve others. Of course, your story is important, and you must process it first and gain your freedom! However, even while you are healing, you can also serve others. The more you think of others, the quicker you will heal.

By being focused on others instead of isolating in your story, you will become even more aware that there is a purpose from your pain. Not that this should have ever happened to you—it shouldn't have! It was never God's desire or will for your life for you to be abused. God is good and He desires good for your life. He is so good that He can take this horrible experience and use it to help others. God knows that when we take the focus off of ourselves (after we have healed), we will no longer be thinking of this horrible experience, but instead will be thinking of the beauty of helping others rise out of the mud and into His marvelous light, as we have!

Obstacles to Healing

As you walk out your healing, don't be surprised to discover that some situations and feelings and thoughts arise that try to block your forward momentum. There are several common blocks that can keep you from moving beyond your hurt and woundedness to the freedom and joy God has for you. By recognizing these obstacles, you'll be equipped and empowered to recognize them and deal with them, so you can be healed.

Obstacle 1: Denial

Denial occurs when we say no to the process of healing. It also occurs when we resist facing the truth of the abuse and its impact on our life. Denial manifests in words like these: "It wasn't that bad." If we think this, then we aren't clearly marking out right from wrong. This is a problem because the abuse will repeat itself in some other area of our life or the lives of our loved ones, because we haven't clearly established what is right and what is wrong.

It also manifests in saying or thinking things like this: "I have no need to process. It didn't affect me that much. I forgave, so it's over." To deny the fact that we need to process a hurt, or that it didn't affect you that much, or that it is over belittles what has happened and puts the abuse in the category that it wasn't that bad.

To counter the obstacle of denial, you need to understand God's desire for your life. You must come to understand and realize that this abusive situation was not how God desired for you to be treated. You also need to understand that you do, in fact, need to go through the process of healing with God, by becoming aware of how abuse or anything contrary to God's will affected you.

Moving out of denial tells us the abuse was wrong and gives us the choice to forgive. Forgiveness is part of the process to healing, it brings peace, and it is a good thing. Be mindful that your journey of healing will be a continual process as you become even more aware of the effects you've experienced from the abuse. Being aware of how it affected you will benefit you and empower you to make the choice to forgive and other choices that bring you a sound mind and a joyful life.

Obstacle 2: Fear

Fear is something we all face in life. It can be uncomfortable to make changes in our lives, even if the changes promise to give us more freedom and more joy. As human beings, we tend to want to stay in our comfort zone since it is familiar to us, rather than making a shift to something new.

For those who have been abused, fear can take on forms like these: fear of facing the truth, fear of feeling emotions, fear of losing control, fear of going insane, and fear of losing a relationship.

To counter these fears, realize that fear is **False Evidence Appearing Real**. The enemy would love to keep you in bondage, so he uses fear as a tactic to hold you hostage, telling you that you are not strong enough to handle the change. But as a child of God, you can *be strong in the Lord and in the power of His might* (Ephesians 6:10 NKJV). You are *more than a conqueror through God who* *loves you* (Romans 8:37). You are here reading this book because you are courageous! You are ready to come against the enemy's lies and to be set free!

Keep in mind that we do not ever have to be afraid of our own feelings. God gave us emotions for a reason. To feel sadness, regret, betrayal, anger, and so on is like a thermometer in our life, showing us that something is wrong, that something needs to be dealt with. Once we address the feelings, we can console ourselves with God's Word and a positive inner narration. We can speak to ourselves like a loving God or loving parent would.

As we work through our strong emotions, we can let ourselves know, "You are right to be angry about this. It wasn't right. I am so sorry this happened. What can we do now to move forward?" We can validate our feelings and at the same time look for good and godly actions we can take to address what we need in a positive and healthy way. When we do this, it eases any fears we have about feeling our feelings.

Remember also that God has given us the ability to have self-control and wisdom. You are here now to learn coping skills and to gain information that will help you process all that has happened. God has not given you a spirit of fear, but of power, love and a sound mind (2 Timothy 1:7). You can and you will overcome!

If you are fearful about losing a relationship, this is understandable. No one likes to lose friends or family. We cannot fear any man over God, the truth of the matter is that sometimes you will lose relationships that are not built on God's love, and those relationships are not worth having. Some relationships will not be able to withstand truth or your healing, and if so, this means these people are not safe people, they are unwilling to face their part in the abuse or someone they may have known that abused you. God wants so much better for you than to have an abusive person in your life, and He will provide you with the right people to be in your life.

Those who are safe and protective, they are healthy, respectful, and have good boundaries, they can appreciate your healing, and desire you to become more like Christ, and to love and care for yourself more.

Obstacle 3: Pride

The Bible tells us that pride goes before a great fall. This is because when we are acting out of pride, we are refusing to receive the things that can make our situation better. Pride says things like this: "I'm fine. I don't need help. I'm never going to break down. I won't be seen weak. I refuse to cry. I won't trust anyone. I can do it all myself."

Notice that pride is all about ego, which is a huge obstacle to healing. To overcome pride, we need to realize that we all need help, and there is no shame in receiving help. We all need encouragement, someone to speak truth into our lives, someone safe to help pull us out of the darkness into God's light. We were not meant to do life alone! By admitting our areas of woundedness and accepting that we would benefit from help of some kind, we are positioning ourselves for success. Accepting help means that we are strong and ready to receive our healing.

Allowing the tears to flow and surrendering to God and safe people in our lives are actions that truly help us to heal. We are letting go of things that do not serve us well. We are opening up space and making room for good to enter our lives! God can only help those who say they need Him. When you're willing to say you need Him, He is there for you! He will be with you and will provide the right people in your life. We can trust Him to lead us to safe people who can truly help us.

Obstacle 4: Negative Attitude

A negative attitude is a considerable obstacle to healing, as it tends to keep us trapped in what isn't working and it moves us away from the positive things that would help us. Negative attitudes can show up in our lives when we are thinking like a victim, allowing negative thoughts, being unaware of how the abuse affected us or is influencing our actions, and not being proactive about doing things that bring about healing in our lives.

To overcome this obstacle, you must first learn to recognize negative-thought saboteurs, which include apathy, blame, criticism, cynicism, depression, dishonesty, fear, guardedness, shame, and more. Once anger has been processed so you can learn what it is telling you, it is important to replace that thought and emotion with what you would like to feel instead. You will add that to your narration so you can daily reprogram your mind with the good thoughts you desire to have and let the negative feeling go. The mind can only hold one thought, so choose the one that is going to build your life instead of destroying it! Build your life by habitually thinking on the positive!

It's important to refuse to think like a victim. A victim is someone who has no hope, no future. To them, everything is ruined. This is not going to be true for you, because I believe you are going to fight for the life you deserve! You are victorious! You will believe the good that God has in store for you, and you will accept nothing less! If you are having an off day, and everyone does, begin immediately to focus on all that you have been blessed with and the future God has in store for you. Take helpful suggestions such as smile, focus on the good, etc., from others and refuse to fall back into victim mentality!

Remember, your outlook is your choice! You can exert healthy self-control by choosing to embrace a positive attitude and think of yourself as someone who is loved by God and able to make good decisions that work for you. You are no longer a victim, but a person who is gaining greater joy and freedom every day through God and through the work you are doing in this book!

Obstacle 5: Lack of Vision for a Better Future

The Bible tells that *if people can't see what God is doing, they stumble all over themselves; but when they attend to what He reveals, they are most blessed* (Proverbs 29:18 MSG). If we don't have a vision for what God would like to do in our lives, then we have no sense of the goal we're moving toward, and it will be hard to arrive at the finish line.

This obstacle begins when we're not focused on God's truth about who we are and what is possible for our lives. And this lack of vision for a better future makes it hard for us to move forward. We may find ourselves having no goals or purpose, no plan of action for our own healing, no accountability, and no plan to help others.

Godly vision is the most important thing we can have in our life! Our mind can be our greatest friend or our worst enemy! When we use our imagination for good and God's glory, we reap the outcome of those good thoughts. Think of all the beauty that you have seen or felt in your life. Now, create more of that. You can do it because God made you to be a creative person; you just need to take the time to think.

In our coaching ministry and in my personal life, I practice godly meditation. This is a practice of sitting quietly for about 5-10 minutes, thinking on all the good things in your life and the good that you would like to create. What does it look like in your mind's eye? What does it feel like? Sound like? What do you hear? Taste? Our senses were given to us as a blessing, to further lock into our mind what we experience. We can also do this with what we have yet to experience and create the actual happening of an event because of what we focus on. *For as he thinks in his heart, so is he* (Proverbs 23:7 NKJV).

Here are some questions for you to ponder and answer as you begin to create an image in your mind of the better future you would like to have.

1. What would you like your future to look like?

   _____
   _____
   _____

2. How will you accomplish these goals?

   _____
   _____
   _____

3. Who will hold you accountable?

   _____
   _____
   _____

4. How will you help others once you achieve your goal?

_____

_____

_____

Gaining Perspective from the Past

We should never compare pain, and we can learn some great lessons on choosing to heal from Lindsey Roy. In Lindsey Roy's Ted Talk called "What Trauma Taught Me about Happiness," which I highly recommend watching, there are some great lessons to be learned.

In her story, Roy shares how a boating accident changed her life forever. It caused an amputation of her left leg and severely injured her right leg. She shares how developing the right perspective was her greatest lesson. She realized that if she continued to focus on the past and thought constantly about what was once "normal life", she would spiral into a dark mindset. She could not change the past. She had to learn how to move and think in a new way with her new prosthetic leg and different life. She had to let go of that yearning of wanting the accident to have never happened and adapt to change so she could live a healthy and happy life.

Roy calls the desire to live a different past a "phantom life"—wanting to live in what should be, instead of living in the now. She wanted her life to be different. She would compare herself to others who had a seemingly better life.

To move forward and find happiness, Roy had to give up the way she felt about loss and change. She began to focus on what she does have and how blessed she is. She learned how forcing herself to think positive thoughts began strengthening her brain and caused her to be happier. She learned to anchor herself to the right perspectives. If she were to compare herself to anyone, she learned to compare her life to those who have it so much worse.

When you are really struggling, ask yourself, what are five ways it could be worse? What are the hidden advantages that came from this situation? When Roy did this, she began to see how her children were more empathetic and caring to others. She realized how she had gained a whole new perspective on life. When she needed encouraging, she would compare day 72 of her recovery to day 7, which helped her to see how far she had come already and how victorious she was becoming.

Roy says we need to choose our mental competition wisely. Our perspective on life can be short-term unless we choose to make it last. She also discovered that she had to detach from her old life and reattach to a new one.

Actively forcing a new perspective on yourself is the best way to be victorious and the cheapest form of therapy. Our way of seeing ourselves and our lives is essential and life-giving if positive, or life-taking if negative. At this point, she says, it is do or die time. Studies have shown that trauma survivors are happier than lottery winners. Survivors have been forced to gain a new perspective. Ask yourself the right questions and see how your view, and you, begin to change.

Like Lindsey you too are gaining a new perspective, a new way of doing life which will be greatly rewarding and will give you a sound mind and a happy life. Because you are anchored to Christ and trust Him to heal you completely you will realize a life filled with great joy and purpose.

A Prayer for You

Dear Lord, I am praying for You to help me to be courageous enough to heal. Help me choose to be whole in You, Lord Jesus. I pray that You teach me how to use godly vision to set good goals, and to build my life instead of tear it down! Help me to focus on Your Word and who You say that I am. Help me to have the right perspective and to focus on all of my blessings. Please provide the right people in my life to hold me accountable to my goals and help me to continually look for my higher purpose in all things. Thank You, Lord, for being with me. In Jesus' name, Amen.

Week 2: Choosing to Heal

DAILY HEALING ACTIVITIES

Write any positive words from these activities in your new godly narration for this week

Day 1: Spirituality

Memorize this scripture:

Heal me, O Lord, and I will be healed; save me and I will be saved, for you are the one I praise.
— Jeremiah 17:14 (NIV)

Questions to help guide you:

1. What are your spiritual goals?

   _____
   _____
   _____

2. What is the purpose of those goals?

   _____
   _____
   _____

For example, some suggested spiritual goals include a closer relationship with Jesus, to be able to hear from Him, to know His will for your life., or to feel His love for you. The purpose for these goals could be to have direction, wisdom, peace, victory, etc.

Day 2: Relationships

Memorize this scripture:

Therefore, if anyone is in Christ, the new creation has come: The old has gone, the new is here! All this is from God, who reconciled us to himself through Christ and gave us the ministry of reconciliation:
—2 Corinthians 5:17-18 (NIV)

Questions to help guide you:

1. What are your relationship goals? List each relationship and get specific.

2. What is the purpose behind these goals?

Examples of relationship goals include to be a good mother, to have a close friend, or to get along with your parents. Purposes for these goals might be to have peace, to feel connected, to have support, etc.

Week 2: Choosing to Heal

Day 3: Emotional Health

Memorize this scripture:

He heals the wounds of every shattered heart. He sets his stars in place, calling them all by their names. How great is our God! There's absolutely nothing his power cannot accomplish, and he has infinite understanding of everything.
—Psalm 147: 3-5 (TPT)

Questions to help guide you:

1. What are your emotional goals?

   _____
   _____
   _____

2. What is the purpose for these goals?

   _____
   _____
   _____

Examples of emotional goals include to be stable and grounded emotionally, to have more joy in my life, or to be able to feel emotion. Purposes of these goals might be to be able to make better decisions, to not feel hurt emotionally, or to be able to connect and understand others.

Day 4: Physical Health

Memorize this scripture:

"But I will restore you to health and heal your wounds," declares the Lord.
—Jeremiah 30:17 (**NIV**)

Questions to help guide you:

1. What are your physical goals?

   _____
   _____
   _____

2. What is the purpose of these goals?

   _____
   _____
   _____

Examples of physical goals include to get healthy, to lose weight, or to have more endurance. Purposes for these goals might include to feel better, to look better, to run a marathon, or to feel victorious.

Week 2: Choosing to Heal

Day 5: Financial Health

Memorize this scripture:

The Lord is my best friend and my shepherd. I always have more than enough. He offers a resting place for me in his luxurious love. His tracks take me to an oasis of peace, the quiet brook of bliss. That's where he restores and revives my life. He opens before me pathways to God's pleasure and leads me along in his footsteps of righteousness so that I can bring honor to his name.
—Psalm 23:1-3 (TPT)

Questions to help guide you:

1. What are your financial goals?

    _____
    _____
    _____

2. What is the purpose for these goals?

    _____
    _____
    _____

Examples of financial goals include to save $25 a week, to purchase a car, to have money for rent, etc. Purposes for these goals include to have an emergency fund., be able to get to work, feel comfortable in your home, etc.

Day 6: Career and Serving Others

Memorize this scripture:

Take delight in the Lord, and He will give you the desires of your heart.
—Psalm 37:4 (NIV)

Questions to help guide you:

1. What are your career goals?

2. What are the purposes for these goals?

Examples of career goals include to go to college to study _____, to be a receptionist, to work as a dental hygienist, etc. Example purposes for these goals include to feel fulfilled, to help others, to make an income, etc.

Week 2: Choosing to Heal

Day 7: Sabbath Rest

Memorize this scripture:

He gives strength to the weary and increases the power of the weak.
—Isaiah 40:29 (NIV)

Do something to relax and restore yourself today!

Some suggestions for self-care include:

- Exercise in your favorite way — walk, jog, skate, do yoga, etc.
- Visit a favorite place to eat and order your favorite meal.
- Take time to visit with a friend and enjoy a cup of tea or coffee.

Write Your Inner Narration

Using what you have learned from this chapter, the scriptures you have memorized this week, and what you discovered while answering this week's questions, build on your original narration from week 1 and write an additional short godly narration using only positive words.

Example: I am loved by God. I am filled with godly purpose. I am equipped and able to achieve my godly goals…etc.

Week 3
Getting to Know the Real You

*For you formed my inward parts; you knitted me together in my mother's womb.
I praise you, for I am fearfully and wonderfully made.*
— Psalm 139:13 (ESV)

Tabitha went through a divorce three years ago and is still feeling such great loss. Shaken to her core, she has no idea how to begin her "new life" as a divorcee. Her marriage had given her a sense of identity. For eight years, she was known as Jim's wife. They had a home and she felt somewhat stable in her married life. Alone now, in an apartment only an hour away from her old life, she is unable to adapt to her "new self." Unable to get over the love that she felt in the beginning with her ex, she still finds herself lingering in the past. She blames herself for the end of her marriage. She "knows" it was because she could never be for him who he wanted her to be. She "knows" she was and is "tainted," that she is "damaged goods" and will never be who she should have been. Would she ever get over it? Would she ever adapt to her "new life" and her "new self?" She doesn't even know who she is. Did she ever?

Tabitha had the false notion that she was who she was because of her marriage. She had a belief about herself being damaged goods because of her abuse. Trauma and life experience formed her beliefs about herself, creating who she identifies herself to be. She has been unable to heal from trauma and divorce because of a lack of knowing her own, true, God-given identity.

Only as we discover who we are can we be healed of past hurts, freed from lies we have mistakenly believed about ourselves, and begin to experience a joyful, purposeful life.

Discovering Who We Are

The search for our true identity is an important part of the healing process, because identity lends itself to purpose and purpose gives vibrancy to living. We must know who we are as individuals, who we have been created by God to be, so we can fulfill our destiny with joy.

It's not unusual for this to feel like a challenge at times. Abuse and trauma strip away our identity in a very dramatic and impactful way; our sense of safety and peace of mind are dramatically altered. We can lose our joyful embracing of the world, of ourselves, and of God. Many emotions such as fear, sadness, guilt, anger and confusion have come pouring into our life as a result of what we went through. These feelings and thoughts can distort how we see ourselves, causing us to let go of things that once mattered to us or to hold onto things that are not helpful to us.

Additionally, there are other events and patterns in our normal lives that also wreak havoc on our identity. How we were raised, our current relationships, marital status, religion, lifestyle, belief systems, and many other things from this life can eventually creep into a belief we develop about who we are, causing us to become confused about our identity. We all benefit from growing and learning more about ourselves and who we are meant to be. You are not alone in this process of self-discovery that each and every one of us must go through.

Who You Really Are

Your feelings and thoughts tie into your beliefs about who you are and what you can accomplish. That means who you believe you are will help you to manage your feelings and think positively about yourself and your future. This is why having a strong sense of your true identity matters so much.

Let me give you a basic definition of identity to begin our discussion. Your identity is:

1. A set of characteristics by which you are definitively recognizable or known.

2. The set of behavioral or personal characteristics that make you recognizable as a member of a group.

3. The quality or condition of being the same as something else.

4. Your distinct personality—your individuality, what makes you uniquely you.

5. The relations established by psychological identification — in other words, what is in your mind about who you are.

Another great way to look at this is that the "real you" is *anything that is positive that God says about you*. Psalm 139:13-14 (NIV) says, *For You (God) created my inmost being; You knit me together in my mother's womb. I praise You because I am fearfully and wonderfully made; Your works are wonderful, I know that full well.* God created you to be the "real you" from the moment you were conceived, and He has a plan for you that He established from the very beginning of your existence. Long before any person in the world knew you, God knew you, and He loved you! And He still loves you!

As a Christian, you belong to God. Everything good He says about you is true, even during the times you may not feel like it. This is why it is important to know who God is and what He has to say about you. (There is a list of "Who I Am in Christ" scriptures in the Appendix that you can use as you learn more about the wonderful, loved, successful, purposeful person you are, which is who God has created you to be!)

Just about everything in life changes. Our feelings change, relationships change, we age, we take new jobs, we move—even our life on this earth is temporary. What, then, is eternal? What never changes? God!

God is eternal. And He becomes our true identity when we are adopted into the family of Jesus Christ. *For He chose us in him before the creation of the world to be holy and blameless in His sight. In love He predestined us for adoption to sonship through Jesus Christ, in accordance with his pleasure and will* (Ephesians 1:4-5 NIV).

Having our identity placed in Jesus Christ gives eternity to our lives. It gives us a place to be rooted, a place that does not change because God doesn't change. When we know that our eternity rests in Jesus, we can become like Paul in the New Testament who was able to be content in all circumstances (Philippians 4:12). Just as we discussed in Week 1, we are each a part of the Big God Story, and because of that, we can know and understand our purpose in this life. We can adopt the characteristics of Christ and gain the knowledge of who we are in Him and thus believe about ourselves who He says we are.

> *Therefore, if anyone is in Christ, he is a new creation.*
> *The old has passed away; behold the new has come.*
> — **2 Corinthians 5:17 (ESV)**

Establish your identity with the One who created you. Jesus Christ loves you and has good plans for you! He will restore your true identity to you! He will give you power from His Holy Spirit to make the changes necessary for you to walk out and live in your true identity! He calls you His child, and He loves you more than you can ever imagine!

I encourage you to visualize yourself in your true identity, which is every aspect of Him—kind, full of light and love, forgiving, radiant, pure, holy, wise, discerning, kind, patient, filled with purpose and so much more. That's who you really are, and who you have always been meant to be.

Letting Go of False Identity

As you move toward complete healing from abuse and trauma, you not only are stepping into your true identity, but also are letting go of what is untrue, the lies you have come to believe as a result of what you experienced.

A false identity is anything that is *not* good. Remember, everything good comes from God (James 1:17). He made you good, with good characteristics, good passions, good habits, a good identity in Him. Therefore, if anything arises in your life that is not good, you can be assured it is a false identity.

If you are believing something bad about yourself, it is a false identity and not of God. If you are acting poorly, these behaviors are coming from a place of false identity.

Keep in mind that the enemy wants to keep you stuck in the past; he is like a roaring lion, trying to make you fearful and distracted. The Bible says, *Stay alert! Watch out for your great enemy, the devil. He prowls around like a roaring lion, looking for someone to devour. Stand firm against him, and be strong in your faith* (1 Peter 5:8-9 NLT). The enemy does not want to see you succeed! He'll try to convince you that you cannot change, and that there is no hope for you. This is a lie!

The truth is that you are stronger than the enemy because you have the Holy Spirit living in you, which makes you wiser and more powerful! *The one who is in you (God) is greater than the one who is in the world (the enemy)* (1 John 4:4 NIV). With God, you can stand up to the enemy and gain your freedom and healing!

You Matter!

Often, abuse and trauma cause us to tell ourselves that we don't matter, that our stories don't matter, and that we are not worthy to take action to better our situation. In fact, one of the reasons that people fall into depression is that they feel out of control of their life. Feeling responsible for what happened to us can cause us to get stuck in the past, thinking we deserve to suffer.

While you don't want to belittle what happened to you, it does not benefit you to stay stuck. Understanding the impact of the abuse on our thoughts and feelings helps us to understand how we can begin to embrace the changes that will make our lives better. As we discover these effects of abuse and begin to address them, we can put ourselves on the path to having a sound mind and happy life. You do not want to be the cause of your own problems! Through God, you have great control over your life—and you are going to use that control to create the life you desire! With God, you cannot help but discover the real you and live the abundant life He intended for you to enjoy.

Because of the abuse you experienced, you may find that negative words, images or sounds often replay over and over in your mind, affecting your emotions and beliefs. This, in turn, affects your decisions and alters your ability to set and keep goals. You might even feel like you've forgotten or lost touch with who you were before the abuse or trauma. I want you to know that this is so very normal for all people. Each and every one of us will experience some form of trauma in our lifetimes, and we'll go through forgetting who we are or wishing we could go back to certain times in our life and undo certain things.

Thankfully, God knows exactly who you are and who He created you to be! He never forgets! And He has created you to be someone who is valuable, successful and joyful. He intercedes for you and prays for you constantly to come into your true identity and who He created you to be. As you come to Him daily, asking Him how the abuse impacted you and who He desires for you to become, He will answer. He will give you a sense of what your next steps should be, and you can begin creating the good life He intended for you!

Rediscovering Your True Identity

Your role now is to discover who you really are, the person God made you to be from the very start. To help you make that discovery, you might consider it like this:

If you were to put yourself in a time machine and go 200 years into the future, where everyone you know and everything you have is gone, who would you still be? What would still be true about you, even if everything else is changed? What would you still be passionate about? What would you love doing? Would you love baking? Would you love running or walking? Would you enjoy painting or drawing or playing an instrument? Would you want to teach children, or help adults get better jobs?

Do you have a sense of who you are after picturing yourself this way? There are other questions you can begin to consider too. Take a little time to think about and write down your answers to these questions:

- What are some of the lies I have believed?
- What kind of personality do I have?
- Does that personality conflict or agree with who God created me to be?
- What kind of personality would I like to have?
- What is my opinion about things I care about?
- What do I like to do? What skills and gifts do I have?

The answers to these questions can help you realize more about who you are, what you think, and what you really love to do when you're given the opportunity to do it. These passions you have clue you into the purpose God has for you, and who you really are in Him. As part of your healing process, you are putting yourself in a position to do these things. You are giving yourself the opportunity to be the real you, and pursue your passions and goals with purpose and success!

Avoiding Self-Sabotage by Taking Control of Feelings

To move forward, you must first take inventory of your thoughts, feelings, and everyday activities. Begin to notice what feelings get in the way of you having a peaceful day. Keep in mind that negative thoughts are what create feelings that cause one to self-sabotage their life! Our mistaken beliefs about ourselves create that negative narrator that leads us into self-sabotage, tripping us up as we move toward our goals.

The good news is, you have control over what you think, feel and do! You can learn where you are sabotaging yourself and how to address it so you can become more successful at reaching your goals. As you come to recognize aspects of your being that are not the real you, and discover who you are all over again, you can begin to set goals that fit with who you really are and what you want to accomplish.

We also have to continue to identify the feelings we have that are based in our past abuse, and the lies we have come to believe, because the lies we tell ourselves and the feelings those lies create in us can get in the way of our healing and our success in life. Let's look at managing feelings, and then we'll look more at our true identity in Christ.

Identify Your Feelings, Then Decide What to Do with Them!

Often, when we have gone through abuse and trauma, we have also learned the coping skill of stuffing down our feelings, so much that it is possible not to recognize anymore what we are feeling and why. In the Appendix, there is a Feelings Chart with related questions you can review to help you identify how you feel at any given time. This skill is important in understanding ourselves, improving our relationships, and accomplishing our goals. Without it, we'll begin to sabotage ourselves and impede our own success.

Keep in mind also that feelings shift and change. They provide you with important information in the moment about what you are thinking and what you may need to do. For this reason, it is very helpful and healing to learn to identify how you feel, where a feeling is coming from, whether or not you can trust those feelings, and how you would like to respond.

Let's take a look at how to go through the process of discovering and working through your feelings. I recommend you practice this as needed, daily. You can even use this whenever you want or need to know how you feel about something. As you process your feelings to work through them and be healed, ask yourself these questions that allow you to understand the feeling more clearly:

- **How am I feeling? What am I feeling?** Here is where the Feelings Chart in the Appendix can really come in handy! Look at the chart and see if you can pick the word or words that fit how you feel right now. Write down the word on a piece of paper or in a journal. For example, you may be feeling angry at how you were abused. You would write down the word "anger."

- **Is this feeling showing me a truth about me? Is this a truth about a situation?** One thing that happens when you have not yet processed old feelings from past events is that you can feel those feelings in situations that remind you of what happened. Ask yourself what is causing you to feel anger in the given moment. For example, are you angry because the person you are talking with looks like your abuser? Are they being abusive in their speech or actions? Are you angry about something that happened earlier in the day, but you are feeling it now because you didn't deal with the anger when it first came up?

- **What do I want to feel? What is the reason I want to feel _____?** In our example, if you are feeling angry, you might ask yourself what you'd prefer to feel instead. Answers might include forgiveness, peace, love, etc. You might also feel out of control when you're angry, and you'd prefer to feel in control.

- **How can I get to the feeling I desire?** Once you are clear about what you'd prefer to feel, you can ask yourself about action steps. Examples might be: Do I need to write? To pray? To read the Bible? Go for a walk? Meditate on the feeling I desire? In the case of anger, activities like journaling and exercising to work up a sweat can also be helpful.

- **What does the feeling I desire to have look like?** This is another great question to help you process what you are going through, so you can arrive where you would like to be. For example, if your goal is to not be angry and instead feel peace, you can consider what peacefulness means to you. What does it feel like? Who do you know who feels that way? What do they look like? Act like? Begin to model that behavior, that look. Feel it on yourself, and you will begin to transform.

One quick note here: Forgiveness is not the same thing as reconciliation or trust. You can forgive someone without opening your life back up to them, especially if the other person is not a safe person. Setting appropriate boundaries is important. We'll discuss this idea in more detail in Week 4.

Choosing Who You Want to Be

In addition to discovering the false identity you may have developed due to abuse and trauma, you also have the opportunity to choose who you will be from now own. You can decide what characteristics you want to be known for. Questions like these can help you with this:

1. What behaviors would you like to possess?

2. What would you like people to say about you, when all is said and done?

3. When you are known as being like someone, would you like that someone to be Jesus Christ?

4. What distinct personality or habits would you like to develop as being a part of who you are, and who you want to be known for?

5. Most importantly and the answer that will determine all the rest: What do you want to believe about yourself?

Remember, what you believe about yourself will determine how you feel, how you interpret your circumstances, and the decisions you make. It is so important to figure out the negative beliefs and lies that you have come to have, so you can begin to change them for the better!

A Prayer for You

Dear Lord, I pray right now for You to help me to continually grow in the knowledge of who You are, and who I am in Christ. Help me to see myself as You see me—as Your well-loved, valuable child who has hope and a bright future filled with purpose. As I work on my healing this week, show me where I currently am in the six key areas of my life. Give me greater vision for where I want to be, and help me to create good plans to get there. Thank You, Lord, for loving me, seeing me for who I am, and helping me to be more like You. In Jesus' name, amen.

Week 3: Getting to Know the Real You

DAILY HEALING ACTIVITIES

As you begin to plan for your goals, you must first know with all your heart that God loves you and desires to give you life! The thief is the one who sought to take that away. *The thief comes only to steal and kill and destroy; I have come that they may have life and have it to the full* (John 10:10 NIV). In addition to knowing that God loves you, you must also come to know that He created you to do great things! *For we are God's masterpiece. He has created us anew in Christ Jesus, so we can do the good things he planned for us long ago* (Ephesians 2:10 NLT).

This week, meditate on one scripture a day regarding your plans for where you'd like to be in each area of your life. Memorize the scripture. Commit your plans to God, and you will prosper!

Reminder: Write any positive words from these activities in your new godly narration for this week.

Day 1: Spirituality Plans

Memorize this scripture:

Commit to the Lord whatever you do, and He will establish your plans.
— **Proverbs 16:3 (NIV)**

Questions to help guide you:

1. Where am I now spiritually?

2. How can I get to where I want to be spiritually?

3. What daily habits would I need to have?

4. What am I willing to sacrifice to achieve my goal?

   _____
   _____
   _____

5. Who can help me get to where I need to be?

   _____
   _____
   _____

6. What resources can I use to get there?

   _____
   _____
   _____

7. How can I help others improve spiritually?

   _____
   _____
   _____

Week 3: Getting to Know the Real You

Day 2: Relationships Plans

Memorize this scripture:

For I know the plans I have for you, declares the Lord, plans to prosper you and not to harm you, plans to give you hope and a future.
— Jeremiah 29:11 (NIV)

Questions to help guide you:

1. Where am I now relationally with_____? (Begin with your relationship with God. Then think of the relationship you have with yourself. For the other relationships in your life, focus only on the healthy ones at this time. Ask God which ones those are. The next chapter is on boundaries, and we will work on your difficult relationships then.)

2. How can I get to where I want to be relationally with_____?

3. What daily habits would I need to have? (examples: affirmations, prayer, writing a nice text daily, speaking life over them 3 times a day, serving, and so on)

4. What am I willing to sacrifice to achieve my goal?

5. Who can help me get to where I need to be? (examples: God, mentors, safe people)

_____
_____
_____

6. What resources can I use to get there? (examples: The Bible, relationship books, songs, affirmations, speaking life over yourself and them, and so on)

_____
_____
_____

7. How can I help others improve relationally? (examples: point them to Jesus, teach others what you have learned—get specific with what that is)

_____
_____
_____

Week 3: Getting to Know the Real You

Day 3. Emotional Health Plans

Memorize this scripture:

Plans fail for lack of counsel, but with many advisers they succeed.
— **Proverbs 15:22 (NIV)**

Questions to help guide you:

1. Where am I now emotionally?

　

2. How can I get to where I want to be emotionally?

　

3. What daily habits would I need to have?

　

4. What am I willing to sacrifice to achieve my goal? (examples: give up speaking negatively about myself and others, give up a bad attitude, going to bed late, eating junk food)

5. Who can help me get to where I need to be? (examples: God, mentors—get specific with the people you name here)

   _____
   _____
   _____

6. What resources can I use to get there? (examples: music, scriptures, positive books, beautiful photos)

   _____
   _____
   _____

7. How can I help others improve emotionally? (examples: speak life over them, teach them what I have learned—again, get specific with the details)

   _____
   _____
   _____

Week 3: Getting to Know the Real You

Day 4. Physical Health Plans

Memorize this scripture:

Let the morning bring me word of your unfailing love, for I have put my trust in you. Show me the way I should go, for to you I entrust my life.
— Psalm 143:8 (NIV)

1. Where am I now physically?

2. How can I get to where I want to be physically?

3. What daily habits would I need to have?

4. What am I willing to sacrifice to achieve my goal?

5. Who can help me get to where I need to be?

   _____
   _____
   _____

6. What resources can I use to get there? (examples: nutrition books, exercise books, and so on)

   _____
   _____
   _____

7. How can I help others improve physically? (examples: exercise with them, teach them about nutrition, and so on)

   _____
   _____
   _____

Week 3: Getting to Know the Real You

Day 5. Financial Health Plans

Memorize this scripture:

The plans of the diligent lead surely to abundance, but everyone who is hasty comes only to poverty.
— **Proverbs 21:5 (ESV)**

Questions to help guide you:

1. Where am I now financially?

   _____
   _____
   _____

2. How can I get to where I want to be financially? (examples: work hard, take an extra job, save)

   _____
   _____
   _____

3. What daily habits would I need to have? (examples: writing everything down that I spend and make, review my finances daily)

   _____
   _____
   _____

4. What am I willing to sacrifice to achieve my goal? (examples: time, spending money on things I don't need—get specific)

   _____
   _____
   _____

5. Who can help me get to where I need to be?

   _____
   _____
   _____

6. What resources can I use to get there? (examples: books on budgeting, books on saving, etc.)

   _____
   _____
   _____

7. How can I help others improve financially? (examples: teach them what I have learned, encourage them to save, take a class, etc.)

   _____
   _____
   _____

Week 3: Getting to Know the Real You

Day 6. Career and Serving Others Plans

Memorize this scripture:

The wisdom of the prudent is to discern his way, but the folly of fools is deceiving.
— Proverbs 14:8 (ESV)

Questions to help guide you:

1. Where am I now in my career? In serving others?

2. How can I get to where I want to be? (examples: go to school, read, get to know people in the field I desire)

3. What daily habits would I need to have? (examples: get up an hour early to study, look for volunteer opportunities, etc.)

4. What am I willing to sacrifice to achieve my goal? (time, money, etc.)

5. Who can help me get to where I need to be?

   _____
   _____
   _____

6. What resources can I use to get there? (books, school, internet, and so on)

   _____
   _____
   _____

7. How can I help others improve in their career and in serving others? (examples: encourage them, teach what I have learned)

   _____
   _____
   _____

Week 3: Getting to Know the Real You

Day 7: Sabbath Rest

Memorize this scripture:

May He give you the desire of your heart and make all your plans succeed.
— Psalm 20:4 (NIV)

Do something to relax and restore yourself today!

Some suggestions for self-care this week include:

- Spending time in an activity you loved as a child, such as reading a good book, drawing, coloring, or finger-painting
- Spending some time enjoying a favorite spot (shop, restaurant, beach, park) and just seeing and listening and taking it all in
- Have some quiet time to pray and meditate on a favorite scripture
- Visit with a friend
- Treat yourself to a favorite snack
- Bake some cookies
- Enjoy a warm bath

Week 3: Inner Narration

Using what you have learned from this chapter, the scriptures you have memorized this week, and what you discovered while answering this week's questions, build on your original narration from earlier weeks and write an additional short godly narration using only positive words.

Example: I am loved, I am part of the family of God, I can do all things through God who gives me strength, I have a great life and a great future…etc.

Week 4
Getting to Know Your Boundaries

The boundary lines have fallen for me in pleasant places; surely I have a delightful inheritance.
I will praise the Lord, who counsels me; even at night my heart instructs me.
— Psalm 16:6-7 (NIV)

Josephine loved John, she thought. After all, John was the father of her child and told her he loved her as well. He said he had "only" raped her one time and that he would never hit her again. She wanted to believe him, and she did at times. He was a broken person, after all, and wasn't she called to love him?

Codependent people such as Josephine have great empathy for others. And empathy is a positive quality when it leads us to take healthy actions in a healthy way with safe people. When we are compassionate within proper limits, we can better avoid abusive, hurtful people and will not burn ourselves out trying to fix people who need to work on fixing themselves.

Misguided compassion can also greatly confuse things when we are in a relationship with an unhealthy person. It can lead us to make poor decisions, become exhausted, and find ourselves in situations that put us at risk of some form of harm.

To protect ourselves and use our empathy and compassion in proper, healthy ways, we must have clear limits to what we will and won't allow. We call these limits "boundaries," and they are crucial to helping us live with joy, purpose and success.

If we have never learned what boundaries are and what they do to empower us to live successfully, we will become lost in the tangle of our unhealthy relationships and situations. This enmeshing makes it difficult to understand where the healthy lines fall. And it can lead us into repeated pain and difficulties, rather than God's best for our lives.

What Are Boundaries?

What are boundaries, and how do we establish them in our lives so that we can live with clarity and peace?

Boundaries are a way of clarifying what is my part and what is yours—what I should and will take ownership of and what someone else should and will take ownership of. Boundaries determine where we draw the line. They are markers that empower us to do what works for us, allowing us to give without giving too much, enabling us to care without becoming codependent, and allowing us to live our lives in ways that keep us healthy.

Boundaries Mean Saying Yes *and* Saying No

By their very definition, boundaries mean that we are choosing to say yes to something, which means we are saying no to something else. This is important in today's world, because we are surrounded by messages that tell us that everything is acceptable, that all things are good, that we are free to do whatever we want. But there are always consequences to what we choose, and so it is important to protect ourselves by choosing what is good and godly.

We are told by the world that it is okay to say yes, and that saying no robs us of opportunities. Much of the "fear of missing out" that people have today is centered around the idea that we are "missing out" on something if we say no to it. Boundaries, on the other hand, remind us that not all things are equally profitable and beneficial to us, so therefore we have a right to choose the things that will lead us to godly success. We will not miss out on God's best for our lives, because we are honoring Him by saying yes to Him and His plan for our lives.

Even God Himself has boundaries, and those boundaries show Him saying yes to what is good and saying no to what is not. For example, in Matthew 10:32-33 (NLT), Jesus says, *Everyone who acknowledges me publicly here on earth, I will also acknowledge before my Father in heaven. But everyone who denies me here on earth, I will also deny before my Father in heaven.*

Jesus is saying that by acknowledging and saying yes to Him as God, you will be saying no to all other gods. He will therefore acknowledge and say yes to you because of your boundaries, but if you do not have boundaries and say yes to all, you are basically denying Jesus. To say yes to Him means you must say no to what is not of Him. This is just one example of how when we say yes to one thing, we are saying no to other things. And it is good to do so. It's the right thing to do!

When we say yes to being healthy, we say no to things like abusing drugs. As we say yes to losing weight, we say no to overeating ice cream. Perhaps we say yes to fruits and vegetables, while saying no to too many fried foods. When we say yes to marriage, we are saying yes to only one person to be our intimate partner, while saying no to all others.

When we understand that saying no to what leads us away from our goals means saying yes to what is good for us, it will make setting boundaries easier. Knowing this is empowering! It allows us to make good choices for ourselves, knowing that we are choosing what is good for us and what brings us closer to our goals.

Learning to Voice Our Boundaries

Knowing and setting boundaries gives you clarity about how you want to live your life, and also makes it clear to those you are in relationship with what you'll permit and what you won't permit.

Boundaries are especially important for people who have been through abuse, since by its very definition, abuse is a violation of boundaries. Whether or not you recognized the abuse as a violation when it occurred, you now know that abusive behavior crosses boundaries, going against your will, and denying your voice. When you lose your voice, which is your ability to speak up for yourself and defend your rights and say no—that's when problems begin to arise.

It can be challenging at first for those who have experienced abuse to speak up for themselves. You may feel at times as though you can't clearly voice what you want. You may still be discovering what it is that you do want. You may feel like you are swinging from too far to one side and then too far to the other. Voicing what you desire can seem hard, painful, scary, and sometimes too harsh. All of this is understandable.

This is why awareness of yourself and what is true for you is huge! When something happens that violates a boundary of yours, give yourself permission to take time and examine what you are feeling. Remove the pressure to respond immediately. Take a few moments to check in with yourself and with God to see what is really happening. Think about what has happened and what the issue is, so that you can then address it. This will help you find your voice and express yourself in ways that are good for you.

It is very important that as you heal, you work on regaining your voice and establishing your desires and limits with confidence. The only way to be treated as the valuable person you are is to have clear boundaries that you articulate well to others, so that people know what you will and won't allow. Boundaries tell people that you know what you're worth, and that you expect to be treated that way. And they empower you to respect yourself and value yourself as well, which is most important!

Setting Boundaries in Every Area of Life

This week, you will look at each of the six key areas of your life and determine what your boundaries are in each of them. Every area of your life has value and needs direction and goals with proper limits so that you can have a sound mind and a happy life. Each area needs your time and attention to thrive. As you set boundaries in each area of your life, you will find yourself with more time and peace, making your life more fulfilled.

Remember, you are the designer of your life. You get to determine what you want in and out of your life, as well as who you will become. You get to decide if you are going to follow the Lord and adhere to His principles, and you get to decide how you will let others know that. These decisions take time, so give yourself permission to take time with each of these areas this week. Focus on just one area per day so you can fully design the life you want to have.

Spiritual Boundaries

*So above all, guard the affections of your heart, for they affect all that you are.
Pay attention to the welfare of your innermost being, for from there flows the wellspring of life.*
— **Proverbs 4:23 (TPT)**

As believers in Christ, we desire not to pollute ourselves with the toxicity of this world, so we have to be careful about what we will permit into our lives. We have to guard our bodies, our minds and our spirits. As a human being, you have rights that include making choices about what you will allow into your life! As a child of God, you have not only basic human rights but also spiritual rights, with the power bestowed upon you by the Holy Spirit to enforce those rights!

Let's start by establishing what your spiritual boundaries will be. What lines will you draw and where will you place your "no trespassing" signs in your spiritual life?

This all begins with your relationship with your Father God. He is the only one person who is all loving, and who always has all of our best interest at heart. After all, He created us so He could be in a relationship with us, and because He loves us, we can trust Him to wisely, lovingly direct what we will do with each area of our lives in ways that are supportive and safe.

This relationship with God begins when we make the choice to invite Him into our lives. Have you asked Jesus to come in and be your Lord? If you have, you have made one of the safest and wisest decisions for yourself that you can ever make. God will keep you safe and will give you wisdom and direction for all the areas of your life. (If you haven't and would like to do so, there's a simple prayer in the Appendix you can use, and you can pray right now to ask God in. It's that easy!)

As you are increasing in your spiritual walk with the Lord, begin each day in His Word. Ask Him during your prayer times to reveal more and more to you about what His will is. As you learn His will for your life, it will become easier to set boundaries that are in line with His plans for you. *Observe what the Lord your God requires: Walk in obedience to him, and keep his decrees and commands, his laws and regulations, as written in the Law of Moses. Do this so that you may prosper in all you do and wherever you go* (1 Kings 2:3 NIV). This is what leads to an abundant and fulfilled life!

As we obey God more and more, He will speak to us more and more, and we will recognize His voice more clearly. If we do not listen to Him, we run the risk of Him not speaking because He has already told us what we need to do. For example, God has told us already that our body is a temple of God and has told us to be clean and sober. If we don't listen to what He has already said in this matter, it makes it more difficult for Him to continue to reveal more information to us.

Spiritual Boundaries Include Our Body, Mind and Spirit

Our spiritual boundaries involve surrendering our entire selves to God; which also includes our body and our mind. God has something to say about each and every area of your life, and He does this for your benefit. Every rule that God has given is for your well-being.

Think about your body, for example, and how you care for it, the foods that you eat. Do those foods nourish your body and help it to feel better? God created nutritional foods for you to eat because He loves you. What about what you drink? Alcohol is not good for the body; it causes all kinds of unhealthy side effects, with being intoxicated one of the most damaging. Water, on the other hand, keeps the body functioning well.

God also has something to say about how you honor your body sexually. He designed sex to be within the confounds of marriage between a man and woman and for it to be sacred and loving. God understands that you were victimized and in no way blames you for that. He will restore purity to you. It is your job to honor the purity He restores you with. If you are someone who has willingly strayed outside the bounds of what God has desired, repent (which means to stop doing that and don't do it again) and ask Him to restore back to you a pure life and He will do that.

Honoring the concept of "the sabbath"—a day of rest once a week—is also a boundary that is good for us to set. According to the Bible, we are to establish one day a week for worshipping God and resting from our labors. Most Christians and churches in the U.S. use Sunday for this purpose. Rest is so very important for our body, mind and spirit. And you can be assured that God desires rest for you, which is why in this workbook we honor what He has commanded and give you a complete day of rest—so you can be restored.

In addition to body and spirit, God has something to say about your mind too. He tells us to take every thought captive (2 Corinthians 10:5). The thoughts we think are very important because they influence how we see ourselves and others, our emotions, and our actions. We can have healthy boundaries for ourselves in this area. As we parent ourselves and make healthy decisions about the boundaries we will keep and adhere to, we reap the benefits of a sound mind and a happy life because of it. With our mind, we also get to decide when we will allow it to rest. A lot of mental exertion can drain us, and it is important to have balance so we will have the energy that we need each and every day.

Remember, saying yes to God is literally saying no to other things!

For example, we set boundaries that involve our spirit and heart, such as how we spend our time. Our time of worship on Saturday or Sunday with fellow believers is a sacred time, and to honor it, we will need to say no to other things that interfere with our worship times, such as watching TV or sleeping in rather than reading our Bible or attending church.

It is not that it is bad to watch TV or occasionally sleep in, but we must learn to discipline ourselves and make good choices that build us up. When we say yes to spending time with God at a church service, or in prayer, we are also saying no to spending that period of time engaged in other activities. Our obedience to God spiritually will necessitate us saying no to other things, such as spending time with people who tear down our beliefs.

The bottom line is that anything that takes you away from God is considered idolatry and is breaking a heart boundary that you have set with yourself for your relationship with God. He is not just another checkbox on our to-do list. This heart boundary is something we make within ourselves. We need to be in charge and determine with God whether something is taking us away from God or bringing us closer to Him. This is why God has instructed us to protect our heart—because it is the wellspring of life (Proverbs 4:23).

Our relationship with Him is the source from which all goodness springs forth in each area of our life. Therefore, setting spiritual boundaries is the most important choice you'll make, and the most rewarding experience that you will ever have!

Relational Boundaries

Do not be misled: Bad company corrupts good character.
—1 Corinthians 15:33 (NIV)

To live well, we must all have boundaries within each and every relationship we have. There are certain things that you will allow, and there are also things that you will not allow: this is a boundary. We should have boundaries not only within ourselves of what we expect from ourselves and will allow into our lives, but also boundaries on those we share life with. This is what helps others to grow and keeps us physically, mentally and spiritually safe and healthy.

Setting strong boundaries with people is often very tricky. This is why it is so very important to have a personal relationship with God so He can direct your path. He will give you peace with your decisions about the boundaries you are setting and who you choose to associate with. What we're focusing on this week is on how to set boundaries with those in your life who are "safe people." We certainly don't keep unsafe people in our close proximity.

What does the term "safe people" mean, and how can it help you to set good boundaries? Safe people are those who are emotionally healthy, spiritually healthy, and mentally healthy. They are people who appreciate your value and worth, and who do not want to do anything that would abuse you in any area. They respect your wants, needs, and opinions. They let you have a voice and invite you to tell them the truth. They are people you can trust to have your best interests at heart. Safe people have good boundaries themselves, and they appreciate and respect the boundaries of others.

Our relationships begin with God. He is the one person you can give free reign to and not worry about boundaries with Him. He is all loving and always, 100% of the time, has our best interest at heart. After all, He made us to be in a relationship with Him because He loves us. He is safe enough to direct what we will do with each area of our life.

Human beings, though, are fallible, and even when we want to have other's best interests at heart, we will make mistakes and be imperfect. For this reason, having boundaries with others is so essential! Clear boundaries do two things that are very helpful in terms of our relationships. Boundaries repel those who don't want to respect you (unsafe people), and they attract people who are capable of respecting you and treating you well (safe people). They allow us to bring into our lives those who can appreciate us without abusing us. It is important to begin building relationships only with safe people, because this will help you to find support and friendship as you heal.

The clearest indicator that someone is mentally, spiritually and physically safe to be around is whether they love God and obey Him. If they do not, it is best to spend minimal to no time with that person. While you may wish to be connected with them, they are not in the right place to support you in your healing process.

Having the desire to spend time with unsafe people in your life, even those who have abused you, may come up because these people are often family members or those you have loved. You may even feel that because you have made the choice to forgive those who have hurt you in the past and abused you, it is okay to then be around them. *It is not.* Not until the individual has been completely reformed through intense counseling and rehabilitation, and there have been safety measures put in place, and even then, it is important to never leave a vulnerable child or person with them. Forgiveness is a wonderful thing that God has given us the ability to do, but it is important to understand that forgiving someone is not the same as trusting them or reconciling with them. We must protect ourselves and others from abusers.

Forgiveness is for us, to set ourselves free from the bondage of bitterness. It is also for the abuser should they come to understand their brokenness. It is helpful and empowering for us to know that we are all broken in some way and if we do not get our healing we will act from a place of brokenness. Your abuser is also broken in some way. You do not need to gain a full understanding of how they were broken, as you will never understand their life completely, but through forgiveness, you are simply acknowledging that you know they were broken in some way, which has caused them to act out hurtfully. Forgiveness empowers you to surrender that person to God's justice so you can have the peace in your life that you desire to have. If forgiveness is something you are still struggling with, go to God and His Word for help. You can also take a specific class and discover more helpful resources on YKIcoaching.com.

Forgiveness is something you do for yourself—to bring you greater freedom and peace. Reconciliation and trust can only happen if the other person is willing to change, which includes seeking their own healing through counseling and allowing God to work in their lives. Many abusers are not willing to do this. And if that's true in your case, you are not obligated to stick by their side. It can be so freeing to be out of a relationship that isn't healthy and doesn't respect your boundaries and your well-being.

Even with safe people, issues can sometimes arise because a boundary has been crossed. We are all human and we make mistakes that need to be addressed. You have the right and the control to choose what limits you are setting and what you will accept. For example, if someone is speaking to you unkindly, you get to decide if you will tolerate this. Just know this: the more you tolerate unkind behavior, the more it will continue. We partner with God and agree with Him about our worth when we do not tolerate unrighteousness. Not tolerating something doesn't mean that you need to be unkind with someone in return. It simply means that you speak in a way that shows you are a valued individual, and then you walk away.

With our children, we love them and would never leave them, especially while they are young. But we can certainly have boundaries with them even when they are young. If they are speaking to you unkindly, you can and should set the boundary that this is unacceptable and then they lose a privilege. We need to set boundaries and do so with kindness! We want to model the behavior we are seeking, which is kindness in this example.

Setting boundaries successfully with other people takes time and practice, and you will become more comfortable with it as you do it more and more, with God's help. It is a process. Using the example of Josephine at the beginning of our chapter, she will first need to discover her worth, and then set boundaries with herself about what she will allow into her body, mind and spirit. This will include her relationship with her husband. She will need to set healthy boundaries that require him to get the help he needs to fully repent of the way he has treated her; he will need to get involved in intense counseling and support groups and be fully reformed in order to build trust back so they can have a healthy marriage. Josephine herself will need to get counseling and have a support group so she can heal. If her husband is unwilling to attend those places of support and change, then she will need to increase the boundaries and follow through with what she has requested.

The follow-through is always the hardest part of enforcing the boundary you have set in place, but when enforced, it will filter what you allow into your life! Your life gets better with a filter. Just as you wouldn't drink dirty water but instead you would filter it and only allow pure water into your body, you must do the same with your relationships so that you can heal and live the abundant life that God intended for you to have.

Whenever you are making a difficult decision on what you will allow into your life, I like to give the analogy of what you would allow into your precious son or daughter's life. We often care more for our children than we do for ourselves. So, think of the loving parent that you are, and ask yourself if you would allow unhealthy people or behaviors into their lives. What answer would you give? Now, parent yourself with that same loving motherly or fatherly tone. Love and respect yourself enough to only allow that which is good and wholesome into your life.

Boundaries even help us to prevent codependency—unhealthy relationships in which one person enables the other. Codependency tends to result from one person in the relationship having taking advantage of the other. Boundaries keep our relationships balanced and allow us to voice and get what we each want and need. Without healthy boundaries, we won't receive what we need from the relationship. We'll give without getting back and end up exhausted and frustrated. Knowing what your limits are and voicing them clearly empowers you to stay healthy and keeps your relationships healthy too, so that you can grow and accomplish your goals.

Emotional Boundaries

So above all, guard the affections of your heart, for they affect all that you are. Pay attention to the welfare of your innermost being, for from there flows the wellspring of life.
—**Proverbs 4:23 (TPT)**

Our emotional pain is primarily caused by our interactions with other people. As a coach, I specialize in emotional wellness, and the number one cause of emotional distress is relationships. This is because emotions and relationships go hand in hand. Therefore, we have to be careful and have healthy boundaries in relationships, so that we will be more able to enjoy emotional wellness.

Additionally, being emotionally well is also determined by our nutrition. You are beginning to see the pattern of how everything in our lives overlaps. When we are not taking care of ourselves nutritionally, it impacts how we feel emotionally. Balance and self-care are important. If all you eat is soda and candy, for example, you will feel depleted because your body isn't getting what it needs. If instead we eat the proteins, fruits and vegetables that God designed for our bodies, then we will feel energized and healthy, causing us to have more joy because our minds are fed the needed nutrition. We will also feel better about ourselves as our appearance reflects the nutrition we have been giving it.

The same goes for getting our exercise and proper amounts of sleep. We have all suffered lack of sleep at one time or other, and it impacts us emotionally. It is simply harder to regulate our feelings when we are tired. And surprisingly, being too sedentary can also impact our emotions, while exercise can help us to shift our emotions into a better place. Studies have shown that sweating can help us to rid our bodies of chemicals released when we are feeling unhappy, and working out can release cortisol, which is a stress hormone and is not good for you, while increasing endorphins which are good chemicals produced by the body that promote happiness and a sense of well-being. Choosing to care for our bodies with sleep and exercise is therefore very important to how we feel.

Our thoughts also impact our emotions. When we are focused on the negative things in life, it impacts how we feel by stirring up our negative feelings—anger, depression, discouragement, resentment, and the like. One way to feel better is to begin by examining what we are meditating on. Meditation is anything you are focusing on and continually thinking on. Are we thinking about what we have been blessed with and feeling gratitude for what is good in our lives right now, or are we focused on all that we don't have and feeling a great void in our hearts? Are you focusing on the past in a healthy way, or an unhealthy way?

It is your choice whether or not you are going to remember what is good or what is bad. You can literally say no to yourself for thinking certain thoughts that are not helpful, empowering or encouraging to you. Just like a loving parent, tell yourself, "No, you are not allowed to think of that."

What about the present moment? Are you feeling blessed and like life is good? Or are you thinking how awful your life is? What about the future? Do you have great faith and trust God, and also predict for yourself that life is going to go great? Or are you caught up in fear and all that could go wrong? You get to choose what you think about for yourself! (We will talk more in Week 5 about how to divinely edit our thinking so we can focus on what is good and godly.)

Our words matter as well. When we speak positive words over ourselves and others, we feel better emotionally. Say no to yourself and choose not to speak anything negative over yourself or others. You will greatly increase your emotional health by setting boundaries on what you will allow in your emotional life.

Physical Boundaries

*Or do you not know that your body is a temple of the Holy Spirit within you,
whom you have from God? You are not your own, for you were bought with a price.
So glorify God in your body.*
— 1 Corinthians 6:19-20 (ESV)

We spoke about our physical boundaries when we addressed spirituality and emotional wellness earlier in this chapter. But here are a few additional ideas to consider. Your physical life matters to God. And because it matters to Him, it should matter to you as well. You are valuable and loved, and that includes your body and physical well-being.

You get to determine your boundaries in your physical life. What habits will you establish to take care of yourself physically? Will you get up early and exercise? When you say yes to physical health, you are saying no to junk food, alcohol, and staying up too late. Instead, you will take care of yourself and go to bed early so you will get the rest that you need. These choices will be well worth it because you are protecting and promoting your own physical health, so that you can enjoy your life.

How you spend your time enters into this area of your life as well. When you set physical time boundaries for yourself, this is known as a schedule. By getting up and going to bed around the same time each day, you make it easier for your body to sleep well. When you eat at regularly set intervals, it's easier to stay on a healthy diet and maintain a healthy weight. When you set planned times to work out, it makes you more successful at creating a habit of getting in your exercise. Simply put, your body will thrive on a healthy schedule.

In addition, you honor your body through morality. Rather than setting yourself up for the consequences of being sexually active outside of marriage, you have the ability to take a purity oath and protect your sexual well-being. This positions you to find the healthy spouse that God intended for you to have.

Financial Boundaries

*Whoever is kind to the poor lends to the Lord,
and he will reward them for what they have done.*
— Proverbs 19:17 (NIV)

Financial boundaries are rules that we put in place over our money. They are important for us, our loved ones and for the poor, and they are something God has instructed us to establish. Remember, God said where your money is, that is where your heart is (Matthew 6:21). Money and the heart are very closely linked.

God has told us to honor Him with our money. *Glorify God with all your wealth, honoring him with your very best, with every increase that comes to you. Then every dimension of your life will overflow with blessings from an uncontainable source of inner joy* (Proverbs 3:9-10 TPT).

When we set aside money to give to the poor and to build up God's kingdom, we are honoring Him. This is known as tithing (giving him a tenth of our income) and offerings (giving Him an amount that is in our heart to give, of any size). As we tithe and give offerings, we show our faith in God, and He honors us when we do this.

God is a generous God, and He always provides. I know this is true for me as I have tithed to God ever since I first came to know Him over 35 years ago, even when I had very little He has always provided for me and has increased my wealth so that I can give to others. In fact, this is a promise He makes in Malachi 3:10 (NIV) — *"Bring the whole tithe into the storehouse, that there may be food in my house. Test me in this," says the Lord Almighty, "and see if I will not throw open the floodgates of heaven and pour out so much blessing that there will not be room enough to store it."*

God has asked us to take care of our money with great wisdom. We are not to spend foolishly on things we don't need or in ways that will not add value to our lives. We are to be prepared to take care of ourselves and our bills, as well as to give to those in need, and the only way to do that is to have boundaries on our finances — which is known as a budget. To say it a little differently, a budget is a boundary that you set on your money. You determine where your money is going and how much you will allow yourself to spend and save. When we place boundaries on how we use our money for ourselves and others, we are using wisdom so that we will not end up with nothing.

You have the right to say no when family members ask you for money. Remember — you matter. Your financial needs matter. Paying your bills and saving for your future matters. We shouldn't take care of extended family members at the expense of our own welfare. By saying no to doing so, you are simply placing a boundary on others for the sake of your financial health.

It may surprise you to think about this, but you do not need a lot of money to budget your money. In fact, it is these boundaries and budgeting your money which will cause you to save and have more money. Of course, one needs to work to make money, so let's talk about career and ministry boundaries.

Career and Ministry Boundaries

*Six days you shall labor and do all your work, but the seventh day is a Sabbath
to the Lord your God, on which you must not do any work.*
— Exodus 20:9-10 (BSB)

God designed for us to have purpose and to work, and He also designed rest. By the very nature of the world and the human beings God created, there is a boundary on both our working lives and our times of resting and recuperating. There is a time in the day to stop and take a break for lunch, a time to stop in the evening and rest, and of course a full one to two days off to rest.

Remember, you are the designer of your life, the one in charge of the boundaries. You get to determine how much you will work, what salary you will accept, and where you will be employed. These choices are boundaries you can set with yourself so that you are in a working environment that supports your worth.

Yes, jobs often decide for us the hours we are expected to work, but we get to decide if we will comply and work the hours the job requires. If the hours, pay or job responsibilities take away from our well-being, we can decide to switch to another job. The choices we make in our working life can and should involve every area of our lives. Our career choices should allow us to support our ability to eat well, to get sleep, to attend our church or spiritual get-togethers sometime during the week, to spend our money wisely, and so on.

Even though we each need to have some form of work, it is unhealthy to work all the time. There is a time to work, and there is also a valuable and needed time to rest (Ecclesiastes 3:1; Exodus 16:23). Rest allows us to take care of our bodies and have time to restore our emotional wellness and meet our spiritual needs too.

Of course, by its very nature, rest has a boundary too, as there is a time to stop resting and begin work again. There is balance to be had in all areas of our life. This is the way God designed us to live, with balance and purpose.

In addition to career and rest times, each of us has a "ministry" to do. Ministry simply means the way we serve others. We are each created to have purpose and to serve others; this is a form of work that we give as a way of honoring the Lord.

Volunteering at church or another organization we appreciate is valuable. But even our service and volunteering must have proper boundaries so that we can be well in every area of life. You get to decide how much time you will spend each week offering your hours for charity. To avoid burning out, we must set boundaries on ourselves and others with the time that we set aside for ministry. Serving others is important, but if we do not place boundaries on it, it will take over our life and become unhealthy.

Seek Balance in All Areas

Remember, balance is key to living a good life! Each and every area of our lives overlaps, and if we stay balanced in every area, we'll find it easier to enjoy a happy life. We need to learn what our boundaries are, so we can convey them to others. Remember what we discussed earlier in this chapter: It is okay to say no! In fact, saying no is essential to maintaining proper balance in our life.

We must practice great soul care just as Jesus did. He took time to pray, to work, to rest, to eat, to spend time with His friends, to attend the synagogue, to preach, and to heal. Because Jesus implemented boundaries in His life and stayed in balance, He was able to live generously with great joy and grace. We can learn from Him and what He has to say about all six key areas of our lives, so that we can live with a sound mind and have a happy life the way He intended.

A Prayer for You

Dear Lord, I thank You for always desiring the very best for me in every area of my life. I ask You today to help me to see areas in my life where I can set boundaries that lead me closer to You and closer to fulfilling my goals, so I can have a sound mind and a happy life. Show me the safe people You have put into position in my life right now, those who respect me and care about me and are strong in the Lord. And help me to quickly recognize those who are unsafe so that I can avoid situations and relationships that would tear me down. Thank You for always being there for me, and giving me strength, courage and joy as I walk closely with You. In Jesus' name, amen.

DAILY HEALING ACTIVITIES

Boundaries are extremely important and come from God! He has boundaries, and His desire is that you too will have the proper boundaries in your life. The questions for the week will help guide you in setting boundaries in each area that are right for you.

Reminder: Write any positive words from these activities in your new godly narration for this week.

Day 1: Spirituality

Memorize this scripture:

"Should you not fear me?" declares the Lord. "Should you not tremble in my presence? I made the sand a boundary for the sea, an everlasting barrier it cannot cross. The waves may roll, but they cannot prevail; they mar roar, but hey cannot cross it."
— Jeremiah 5:22 (NIV)

Questions to help guide you:

1. Have I made Jesus my Lord? (When you make Jesus your Lord, you will say no to other things in your life.)

2. Am I willing to trust and allow Jesus to be my Lord? (When you trust Jesus, you will obey Him, and this means saying no to other things.)

3. What are my spiritual boundaries? (Examples: Spiritually, I only allow PG-13 movies into my life. I do not use drugs or alcohol. I stay sexually pure, etc.)

Week 4: Getting to Know Your Boundaries

4. What (or who) am I saying yes to? No to? (Examples: I say yes to Jesus, and I say no to ungodly things. I am saying no to any form of abuse, no to toxic people in my life. I am saying yes to love and respect, and to healthy people.)

   _____
   _____
   _____

5. What do I need to avoid in order to keep my spiritual boundaries? (Examples: I need to avoid parties involving drugs and alcohol. I need to avoid unhealthy people. Etc.)

   _____
   _____
   _____

6. What would my life look like if I fully trusted God and listened to Him? (Examples: If I fully trusted God, I would go to Him daily and spend at least 30 minutes with Him in prayer and His Word. I would have healthy and safe people in my life who love me and support me. I would exercise and eat healthy. I would be happy and have great peace in my life, etc.)

   _____
   _____
   _____

7. How can I help others keep their spiritual boundaries? (Examples: I will help others keep their spiritual boundaries by encouraging them and speaking positive words over them. Share scriptures with them, etc.)

   _____
   _____
   _____

Day 2: Relationships

Memorize this scripture:

Do not be misled: "Bad company corrupts good character."
— 1 Corinthians 15:33 (NIV)

Questions to help guide you:

1. What relationship boundaries do I have? (Examples: I currently require my child to speak kindly to me. I say no to people that drink alcohol or use drugs, etc.)

2. What relationship boundaries do I need to have? Want to have? (Examples: I need to have boundaries with my boyfriend who is still drinking and can be verbally abusive. I want to limit the time I spend with my parent who is verbally abusive.)

3. Is there anything keeping me from enforcing those boundaries?(Examples: I feel afraid of losing love, of being alone. I am afraid people will think I am mean.)

4. How would my life look in the future if I were to keep my boundaries? (Examples: I would have healthier people in my life. I would spend quality time with those who are trustworthy.)

5. Which people are toxic in my life? (Ex. My friend_____, my mother, father, etc.)

_____
_____
_____

6. Which people are good for me? (Ex. I have nice people at church I would like to know better.)

_____
_____
_____

7. What kind of people do I want to surround myself with? (Ex. I want loving people who will support me and speak to me with kindness.)

_____
_____
_____

8. How can I help others keep their relationship boundaries? (Ex. I can encourage them to love themselves and have respect for themselves. I can speak positive words over them.)

_____
_____
_____

Day 3: Emotional Health

Memorize this scripture:

So above all, guard the affections of your heart, for they affect all that you are. Pay attention to the welfare of your innermost being, for from there flows the wellspring of life.
— *Proverbs 4:23 (TPT)*

Questions to help guide you:

1. What are my emotional boundaries? (Ex. I make sure to get outside each day. I only allow myself to think on that which is good.)

2. What emotional boundaries do I need to have with myself? (Ex. I will not allow myself negative thoughts. If I do, I read an additional chapter in the Bible.) With others? What are the consequences? (Ex. I will not allow others to speak unkindly to me. If someone does, I walk away.)

3. What (or who) am I saying no to emotionally? (Ex. I am saying no to staying up late so I can feel rested. I have to say no to watching TV late with my husband.)

4. What (or who) am I saying yes to emotionally? (Ex. I am saying yes to going to church each Sunday as this nourishes my soul. I am saying yes to talking with my good friend who checks up on me.)

_____
_____
_____

5. What amount of time am I willing to spend to be emotionally healthy? (Ex. I am willing to get up 30 minutes early and read the Bible and pray. I am willing to walk for 30 minutes each day.)

_____
_____
_____

6. What affects my emotions negatively that I need to eliminate? (Ex. I feel emotionally unwell when I think about past traumatic events. I am saying no to myself when the thoughts come up.)

_____
_____
_____

7. What would my life look like with healthy emotional boundaries? (Ex. I would have great peace. I would feel happy and smile a lot.)

_____
_____
_____

8. How will I help others with their emotional boundaries? (Ex. I will smile at others so they will feel loved. I will speak kind words over others and teach them how to say no to themselves.)

_____
_____
_____

Day 4: Physical Health

Memorize this scripture:

Or do you not know that your body is a temple of the Holy Spirit within you, whom you have from God? You are not your own, for you were bought with a price. So, glorify God in your body.
— 1 Corinthians 6:19-20 (ESV)

Questions to help guide you:

1. What physical boundaries do I have? (Ex. I don't allow myself to drink alcohol. I make myself go to bed early.)

2. What physical boundaries do I need to have? (Ex. I need to say no to eating cookies late at night. I need to say no to having sex outside of marriage.)

3. What or who am I saying yes to physically? (Ex. I am saying yes to taking a walk with my husband in the evening.)

4. What or who am I saying no to physically? (Ex. I am saying no to my friend talking with me so late at night that I don't get enough sleep.)

Week 4: Getting to Know Your Boundaries

5. What amount of time am I willing to spend to be physically healthy? (Ex. I am willing to spend one hour on Saturdays shopping for healthy foods.

　

6. What affects me physically that I need to say no to? (Ex. Staying up late at night affects my sleep. Eating too much chocolate causes me to feel sick.)

　

7. What would my life look like with healthy physical boundaries? (ex. I would feel healthy and strong and look fit.)

　

8. How can I help others with physical boundaries? (Ex. I could take a walk with my friend and help them learn about healthy foods.)

Day 5: Financial Health

Memorize this scripture:

Whoever is kind to the poor lends to the Lord, and he will reward them for what they have done.
— **Proverbs 19:17 (NIV)**

Questions to help guide you:

1. What are my financial boundaries? (Ex. I say no to what I can't afford.)

   _____
   _____
   _____

2. What would I like my financial boundaries to be? (Ex. My financial boundaries are going to be that I will save 10% of my income, tithe 10% and spend 80%. I will keep a record of my daily expenses.)

   _____
   _____
   _____

3. What affects my finances negatively that I need to eliminate? (Ex. I need to eliminate spending money on cigarettes. I need to stop spending without keeping a record of what I spend.)

   _____
   _____
   _____

4. What or who do I need to say yes to financially? (Ex. I need to say yes to creating a budget and sticking to it. I need to go over finances with my spouse.)

   _____
   _____
   _____

Week 4: Getting to Know Your Boundaries

5. What or who do I need to say no to financially? (Ex. I need to say no to my mom when she asks for money.)

   _____
   _____
   _____

6. What amount of time am I willing to spend to be financially healthy? (Ex. I am willing to spend 15 minutes daily to review my finances.)

   _____
   _____
   _____

7. What would my life look like with healthy financial boundaries? (Ex. I would feel in control. I would have hope for my future. I would have security and extra money.)

   _____
   _____
   _____

8. How can I help others with their financial boundaries? (Ex. I will teach them how to budget and say no.)

   _____
   _____
   _____

Day 6: Career and Serving Others

Memorize this scripture:

The lines have fallen to me in pleasant places; Indeed, my heritage is beautiful to me.
— Psalm 16:6 (NASB) (Special note: This whole chapter is great, and I encourage you to read it all!)

Questions to help guide you:

1. What are my career and ministry boundaries? (Ex. I don't allow myself to work more than 40 hours a week. With serving others, I need better boundaries.)

2. What would I like my career and ministry boundaries to be? (Ex. I am going to set boundaries on the extra work I take on for fellow employees. I will serve one person for one hour per week. This might be babysitting, helping my adult children, picking up groceries for a friend.)

3. What or who do I need to say yes to in my career and ministry? (Ex. I need to say yes to learning more job skills and fitting that into my schedule. I need to say yes to helping a friend learn job skills.)

4. What or who do I need to say no to in my career and ministry? (Ex. I need to say no to my boss when he wants me to work over 40 hours. I need to say no after I have volunteered 1 hour per week and not feel guilty.)

_____

_____

_____

5. How much time am I willing to spend becoming healthy in both my career and ministry? (Ex. I am willing to spend an extra hour per week learning new skills that apply to both career and serving others.)

_____

_____

_____

6. What would my life look like if I had good career and ministry boundaries? (Ex. I would be happy. I would be well rested. I would have purpose and make decent money.)

_____

_____

_____

7. How can I help others with their career and ministry boundaries? (Ex. I would teach others how to say no, so they do not overwork and find joy in what they do.)

_____

_____

_____

Day 7: Sabbath Rest

Memorize this scripture:

Jesus answered, "Truly, truly, I say to you, unless one is born of water and the Spirit, he cannot enter the kingdom of God."
— John 3:5 ESV

Do something to relax and restore yourself today!

Some suggestions for self-care this week include:

- Take some time to study a skill you've been wanting to learn. Perhaps watch a YouTube video or get a book on the subject from the library.

- Pick a boundary you want to work on, and practice it. For example, if you want to eat healthy meals, find a healthy recipe you have always wanted to try, and make it for yourself and a friend.

- Spend some time enjoying flowers around your home, your neighborhood, or a local park.

Week 4: Inner Narration

Using what you have learned from this chapter, the scriptures you have memorized this week, and what you discovered while answering this week's questions, build on your original narration from earlier weeks, and write an additional short godly narration using only positive words.

Example: I am focused. I am able to communicate clearly and effectively. I am compassionate. I am strong…etc.

Week 5
Changing Your Mindset

Be transformed by the renewal of your mind.
— Romans 12:2 (ESV)

> *Once Kendall began to proclaim over herself who she was and is in Christ, her mind began to reward her with peace. She learned that to continue to dwell on her past was hurting her daily life and causing her even more grief. She discovered that she was turning into an abuser by wounding herself with her own thoughts. It certainly was not easy to surrender her right to think about how she was wronged, but once she made the decision and commitment to walk in victory, her whole life changed for the better!*

This week, we are going to learn more about changing our mindset. We have talked throughout this course about the impact of abuse. We discovered the negative programming that we developed because of abuse. We now recognize so many of the lies we believed over the years—thoughts that did not agree with the truth of our identity in Christ!

We've begun to uncover the negative thoughts of our old narrator—that voice inside our head that tormented us, giving us thoughts of unworthiness throughout the day. If we feel unworthy, we will not be able to stand up for truth and for what we deserve. In other words, so much of what holds us back from accomplishing our good and godly goals is rooted in *what we think*!

So now, we are going to dive really deep on this topic and learn the methods for changing our thought process. Through practical actions such as anchoring, using the "I AM" tool, and using our thoughts, words and imagination, we'll discover how to create the future that we desire.

What Is a Trigger?

You have no doubt heard the expression, "That person is really *pushing my buttons* today." It's a phrase we use to describe a repetitive, unpleasant pattern of thoughts, feelings and actions that arise when a certain person or situation drives us to react negatively. These buttons are also called triggers, and every one of us as human beings has them because of what we have experienced in our past.

For some, a trigger or button might arise from something said, such as every time someone says something snide that reminds us of the disrespect we endured in the past. For others, a trigger might be more heartbreaking, such as feeling sad whenever we see an ambulance because it reminds us of when our loved one was taken to the hospital after a heart attack.

For those who have endured abuse, triggers can be even more traumatic and painful. There can be many things that remind us of the abuse or the abuser. These triggers can be overwhelming to us at times, making it hard to live the life God has given us and enjoy the good things we have in the present moment. But as we learn to recognize our personal triggers and discover how to manage them in better ways by taking control of our thinking and emotions, we can gain more control over our lives, find the healing we desire, and move forward into what is good.

Awareness Is Your Friend

When you know the truth, it truly does set you free. Knowledge is powerful in every area of life, including our own thinking and behaviors, and what triggers them. Most of us are unaware of our triggers, so when we go into panic mode, we can feel confused and hopeless because we don't quite understand what is happening. Awareness of what you are experiencing in your thoughts, emotions and even your body will become your friend—because the more you know about what is driving your thinking and the outcome of those thoughts, the easier it is to recognize the connection and put a stop to it. You will then take control and make the necessary good choices that will give you your desired outcome!

Contrary to what you might have been taught or believe, knowing the details of your trauma is not nearly as important as knowing the triggers that cause you to feel a certain way, often leading you to make poor choices which bring about defeat. You don't need to pick the scab. That act actually prevents healing instead of promoting it. Your body, heart and soul truly desire healing, and knowing how to do so allows the scab to heal and go away. This is why our goal is not to keep reliving our bad experiences, but instead to recognize what is negatively triggering us and learn the tools to counter that stimulant so we can move forward and enjoy our lives.

Triggers can set off PTSD—post-traumatic stress disorder which is a common result of being abused. They bring back strong memories if they are not reprogrammed, which I am going to teach you how to do. Unless you reprogram your triggers into positive ones, you may feel like you're living through your traumatic events all over again. (We'll discuss this more in a moment.)

Triggers also bring with them the lies and the feelings of being a victim. Tormenting you in this way is the enemy's greatest weapon to hurt you. When you know the devil's tactics and the lies, fear and misery he desires to keep you in, it becomes easier to recognize them, respond according to what God says instead, and win the battle! Remember, the enemy is like a roaring lion ready to devour you (1 Peter 5:8). This roaring lion is an *imposter*. The true lion is the Lion of Judah, our Lord Jesus—and He is a protector, ready to devour your enemy!

Know Your Triggers

The first step to reprogramming our negative triggers (or buttons) is to learn to recognize what they are. And they may be different for everyone. One of us might respond negatively to loud voices, for example, while it doesn't even bother someone else. For this reason, it is so valuable to become aware of ourselves and our personal reactions to things. That way, we can begin to take control of what is happening.

Some triggers may be obvious to us, such as seeing a news report or TV show that describes violence or hearing about an assault that happened to someone else. Other buttons and triggers may not be quite so obvious. It may take a little more attention to figure them out. Sometimes, our triggers are coupled with good things, such as a beautiful sunny day if your trauma occurred during that time.

Here's the good news—You get to take back your sunny days and make them beautiful because you are going to become skilled at reprogramming your mind! But first, we need to understand how triggers work.

Very often, triggers include some or all of your five senses—sight, hearing, smell, touch and taste—as well as any thoughts and emotions that remind you of the traumatic event in some way. We learn through our five senses, our thoughts and our emotions. So it's no wonder that our triggers are connected to what we have experienced. During the abuse, your brain attached the details of what happened with fear in order to protect you.

Know the Most Common Triggers

What are the things in your life and environment that tend to push you into symptoms of PTSD, stress, fear and other issues related to the abuse? Are you aware of them? To help you become more aware of what is happening inside you, here are some common triggers that people have:

People: Seeing the person or someone that resembles the abuser.

Touch: Aggressive touching is something that is harmful and is to be avoided at all costs. It is a warning sign to you. On the other hand, touching that should have been safe can be reprogrammed.

Thoughts and Feelings: The way you felt or the thoughts you were having during the time or about the abuse.

Objects: Seeing a similar object that you associate with abuse.

Smells: Alcohol, smoke, colognes, etc. Any smell that you associated with abuse. The sense of smell strongly affects our memory. For this reason, you will learn how to use it in a positive way to reprogram your mind and divinely edit any negative triggers.

Environment: Different locations and scenarios that need reprogramming.

Sight: Be aware of what you watch on TV, movies, news reports, etc. Be careful and kind to yourself. There is never a reason to intentionally watch a movie with a scene that disturbs you. If you are watching with someone and it disturbs you, walk out or turn it off. Be honest with yourself and others—you deserve it!

Remember that God has said in His Word to focus on all that is lovely and of good report. *Finally, brothers and sisters, whatever is true, whatever is noble, whatever is right, whatever is pure, whatever is lovely, whatever is admirable—if anything is excellent or praiseworthy—think about such things* (Philippians 4:8 NIV).

Hearing: Specific sounds, music and even words. These can be reprogrammed, as well as avoided when possible.

Tastes: Alcohol, smoke, food.

Dates: Dates, like all the other triggers, can be reprogrammed. A date on the calendar can never harm you.

As you grow more aware of your own personal triggers, you can finetune this list, adding to it as you need to. And you can then begin to reprogram your personal triggers to create more positive associations and take better control of your mind and your emotions. Remember, *you* are in control of your life. You are in the driver's seat!

When Everyday Life Collides with Post-Traumatic Stress Disorder

As mentioned briefly above, many of us who have suffered abuse, or a traumatic experience also can develop post-traumatic stress disorder (PTSD). There is so much to talk about when it comes to PTSD that we can't cover it all here. Therapy can be beneficial for some, and it is often useful to get trusted advice from those with training in treating PTSD, such as a doctor. For our purposes, we will look specifically at how our triggers are related to PTSD and how reprogramming our mind with God's Word can be a helpful and healing tool.

Past traumatic events can cause troubles in the present if they have not been properly processed. The unprocessed memories are believed to carry with them the emotions, thoughts, and physical sensations that were present at the time of the trauma. With PTSD, because your mind is trying to keep you safe, when you are triggered, your body gets ready to fight, flee or freeze. Your heart beats faster, and your senses go on high alert. You feel unsafe. You may feel frozen or unable to act, even when you know it is to your benefit to do so.

These are normal survival responses in a life-threatening situation. What happens with post-traumatic stress disorder is that our bodies and minds go into survival mode even when it is not necessary. Because of PTSD, you may see, feel, smell, touch, or taste something that brings on your symptoms. When one of these buttons is pushed, your mind switches to a sense of danger, heightened alert, heart palpitations, and a desire to freeze, fight or run. You may experience flashbacks from the trauma. You may feel on edge, fearful, anxious, angry, ashamed, or depressed. You may feel numb or detached. Other reactions that can arise when you are triggered include trouble sleeping, changes in appetite, nightmares, feelings of alienation, inability to express positive emotions, hypervigilance, and even reckless behavior. All these responses are a common result of PTSD due to the trauma you endured.

While triggers themselves are often harmless sensory information (such as the scent of cologne or the sound of knocking at the door), they still may cause your body to react as if you're in danger. When what you learned to associate with danger arises, it is as if the buttons that turn on your alarm system are being activated. Your brain and body stop some of their normal functions to deal with what feels like a threat. This stress can harm our bodies, our minds, and our daily activities, which is why it is so important to reprogram them!

God has given you great wisdom and discernment to know the difference between when you are safe and when you are not. For example, it is safe to reprogram your mind to know that blue eyes are not a threat to you. If, on the other hand, you learned some valuable lessons such as not walking down a dark street alone, let your wisdom and godly discernment keep you safe. Trust God to reveal to you which triggers are false, and if there is possibly true danger.

For many, PTSD can be a difficult challenge that will require strong faith in God, in His Word the Bible and have a willingness to believe in His promises and persevere. God is faithful, and with Him, nothing is impossible! We can choose each day to surrender to God's love, His truth and walk in victory as we stand up against PTSD which allows us to rest in God's grace and compassion. PTSD is not something to ignore, but something to learn from and partner with God in so we can heal from it. We are invited to approach God boldly and to pour out our hearts to Him (Hebrews 4:14–16). We are assured that nothing can separate us from His love (Romans 8:35–38).

God can restore the mental health of the PTSD sufferer. In the end, God can even use the situation for His glory. *For everything that was written in the past was written for our instruction, so that through endurance and the encouragement of the Scriptures, we might have hope. Now may the God who gives endurance and encouragement grant you harmony with one another in Christ Jesus, so that with one mind and one voice you may glorify the God and Father of our Lord Jesus Christ* (Romans 15:4-6 NIV).

Triggers are nothing more than a thought that cannot harm you! They may feel powerful, but you can be in control and create an even more powerful and good life! Negative triggers do not protect us. Choosing to heal, learning boundaries and following God are the things that will truly protect you and give you the good life you deserve. You can and will "deactivate" these faulty buttons in your alarm system when you practice the methods provided to reprogram your mind so you can heal and enjoy great peace.

Healing from PTSD through Reprogramming Triggers

In dealing with symptoms of PTSD, it is important for you to help your mind process the trauma so that it recognizes that it is *in the past*. Otherwise, you will be constantly triggered, thinking you are not safe, when in fact you are. You do not want to feel stressed and frightened even when you know you are safe. It is important to get the past healed and your current state of mind settled with what is true about your safety.

This is what is known as congruency. Congruency is when your mind, heart and actions all work together. It is deep and authentic and connects all three in harmony. Many things need to be brought to the light and healed so that safety, contentment and peace are not only in your mind, but also run deep into your heart, producing peace and healthy actions.

You may wonder how you will know when you have processed your trauma. The answer I like to give is, "When it doesn't hurt anymore." As you work through it and find healing, you will discover that the triggers you once had don't affect you so strongly any longer. Thoughts and memories of the past may come, but they don't linger. The pain no longer throbs and throbs. Instead, you will be able to put the thought to rest. If you are aware of what you need to know and the pain doesn't hurt anymore, there is no more reason to revisit it.

The Tool of Divine Editing

One way we can begin to manage our PTSD symptoms and move past them is through a process I call "Divine Editing." With this technique, we first identify our negative triggers, then identify a positive association to attach to it instead, using one of our five senses to help us. We create a positive trigger that replaces the negative one, divinely editing our minds just like we would a computer document, removing what we don't want and replacing it with what we do want. In this way, each time we come across what used to trigger us negatively will instead trigger us positively. Good thoughts will then become the new association.

Remember, our thoughts determine how we feel. We get to be in control of our thoughts so that we can feel better!

If hearing a certain sound causes you to feel negatively triggered, first comfort yourself, and then begin to replace the negative thought associated with the sound by replacing it with a positive thought for that sound. For example, if a siren going off causes you to reexperience the trauma you endured because you heard sirens during your trauma, you can first begin by listing all of the good things that do happen when this sound goes off.

There is always something good that can be associated with something we have taken in with our five senses. Sirens can signal that rescuers are on their way, for example. Look for those positive associations. Then, replace the negative memory with these positive things in your mind and associate them with the sound. You might role play in your mind this siren saving a loved one. Repeat it over and over again until you naturally get to the point that when you hear the sound, the positive image comes to mind.

Another situation for using this technique would be the physical appearance of anyone who could possibly resemble the abuser—using a beard that may negatively trigger you as an example, delete the bad and then bring to mind all the positive people you know who have a beard. You might even search online for heroes with this look, with key words like "hero with a beard." Then begin programming your mind as often as five to twenty times or more a day, associating a beard with a positive person. Over time, as you do this, when you see someone with a beard, you will naturally think of the good people you know and the positive things they have done.

Transforming Our Triggers

For God hath not given us the spirit of fear; but of power, and of love, and of a sound mind.
—2 Timothy 1:7 (KJV)

Our mind is our greatest tool or our greatest tormentor. It can either work for us, or against us. Think about what makes the difference between having a good day or a bad day. Even in stressful or negative circumstances, it is still all about the mind—what we are thinking about or what we are feeling. We can make situations worse or better by what we choose to focus on, and how we choose to speak to ourselves about what is happening in our lives. This is very normal, and with God's help, we can learn to choose and control our thoughts for our good.

To make changes in our inner narrator, we need to understand and learn how to focus our mind on our true identity in Christ. Remember, if we are feeling powerless, we will find it harder to use our voice and stand up for ourselves. But in Christ, we are powerful! As we know our true identity in Him, we can get on our own team and have our narrator speak to us the way it should—with the positive, encouraging, uplifting words that Jesus would use to speak to us!

In the Appendix, you will find a list of scriptures about who you are in Christ. There is also a list of negative lies people commonly tell themselves, countered by the truth of what God has to say about us in the Bible. Both of these references can be very useful as you learn to think of yourself and speak about yourself as *He* sees you—powerful, beautiful, loved, forgiven, free…and so much more!

As you learn of your true identity in Christ, you will use the technique of "godly meditation" to focus your mind onto that which is true, good and godly. This is how you will train your narrator to speak in a positive, biblical way that will strengthen and benefit you. This tool also helps us to review the things we have experienced in our lives, so we can divinely edit our thoughts and triggers, reprogramming them so that we can be free from the physical and mental stress associated with the trauma of our past and enjoy our life as God intends for us.

Let's do a simple meditation exercise right now to see how powerful our thoughts can be to affect our body and mind.

The Lemon Exercise

Imagine yourself closing your eyes for a moment. Picture yourself in a beautiful kitchen. You feel happy, content and at peace. On the counter, you see a bowl of lemons. You can see the light coming in through the kitchen window, shining on the bowl of lemons. It looks pleasing to you. You smell the clean smell of citrus, something you enjoy. It reminds you of summer, happiness, and joy.

The lemons smell so good that you reach over and grab one from the bowl. You feel the bumpy and oily texture of the skin. It looks so good, you decide you would like to taste the lemon. You cut the lemon in half and tilt your head back and squeeze the lemon into your mouth. The juice is so sour! Your mouth begins to salivate. The sour juice causes you to pucker up, and your mouth begins to water even more!

Now, mentally come back to your open eyes and this moment. The vivid details caused your mind to see, smell, feel and taste the lemon. Just imagining the lemon and its juice in your mouth caused you to have a physical reaction.

Using the Power of the Mind to Transform Triggers

This is how powerful our minds are! What we imagine, we can experience as if it is happening in real life. Our physiology (our body) and our psychology (emotions and thoughts) are all designed to line up with one another. When we smile, for example, our mind tells us to be happy. When we focus on something that we enjoy, our body tells us to smile. This is something God instilled in our very being for our good, and we can use it to help us heal.

Not only that, but it is also true that our minds can only hold one thought at a time. Though it might seem like we are multitasking as we do several things at the same time, this is not really the case. Instead, our mind is simply switching from task to task, perhaps quickly, but it is still focused on only one thing at a time. So, if our mind begins to think about something that is painful, such as a past memory or an emotional response to what someone has done, that is what we will continue to think about—*unless we choose to change our line of thinking.* If we choose instead to redirect our thoughts to something else, our mind can set aside the painful memory or hurtful emotions to focus on our new thoughts.

This explains why it is so important to remain in the driver's seat with what we choose to focus on and think about. The more we take control of our thoughts and focus on the one thought that we decide is best for us, the more we will find happiness. The Bible tells us that a double-minded man will fall (James 1:8). As the brain hops from thought to thought, it becomes exhausting. But the more we choose to direct our thoughts onto that which is peaceful and encouraging, we can begin to change our thinking to what is good and godly and find healing.

We can use this trait of how our mind works to help ourselves transform our triggers through godly meditation and divine editing. We must make this practice a daily habit. This is where creating a new, positive narrator helps us too. We practice daily talking to ourselves in encouraging ways— the ways that God talks to us as His well-loved, precious children. We use our five senses and the technique of divine editing to help us reprogram our triggers and create a new narrator that builds us up and empowers us to live a happy life.

An Example of Transformation

I've used divine editing, with God's help, as a great tool for helping me find healing. For myself, as an example, I experienced bad things associated with Las Vegas in my past, so I used to get negatively triggered by going to Vegas or even just hearing about Vegas. I used to say negative things as a result, such as, "Nothing good ever happens in Las Vegas." But I learned to divinely edit those bad things out of my mind and associate Vegas instead with positive experiences! I did this through my godly imagination, godly thoughts, and lots of work reprogramming!

To do so, I meditated and focused my thoughts on what was and is positive for me about Las Vegas. What did I taste in Vegas that I really enjoyed? The great restaurants—wonderful food that was colorful and delicious! What did I see in Vegas that I appreciated? The beautiful architecture and creatively decorated buildings and rooms! What did I hear that made me smile? Beautiful music from shows I attended, and my children laughing and chatting happily with one another! What did I touch that felt pleasant? My husband's loving embrace, holding my children's hands. What did I smell? Good food, perfume, flowers, and so on.

I let these positive things become so saturated in my mind that they are now what I think about when I hear someone mention Las Vegas. But it was a choice. If left to itself, our mind will want to go to that which is painful and dark. It takes work to redirect our mind at first. But over time, it becomes easier and more natural to us. Sure, we may still have a negative thought that passes through our mind, but it won't linger because we will know how to immediately take it captive (2 Corinthians 10:5).

As you begin to use these techniques to reprogram your thinking, keep in mind the 5 Keys to Success! These will transform every situation and trigger. Remembering the Fifth Key to give back to others is what is going to take the focus off of yourself and place it on caring for someone else. In this way, you will be constantly looking for ways to comfort others with the same comfort that you have received! This is so healthy and encouraging for both you and the people you are giving back to.

Anchoring Ourselves to Produce Positive Emotions

We all have a God-given ability to visualize and prepare ourselves for success. Anchoring is a technique that empowers us to do so. In anchoring, we learn to connect something we experience with our five senses to a positive feeling we desire to have. It is therefore a powerful tool we can use to help ourselves get back to a state of confidence, peace and power in the face of PTSD symptoms. It is also an effective tool that moves us out of the thoughts and behavior patterns we wish to change, so we can move toward the goals we have.

Remember, feelings are powerful. They were given to us by God for a purpose. Feelings can tell us when we are in situations that need to change, and they can persuade us to take action. We just need to be master over those feelings and decide how we want and need to feel. We want our feelings to work for us. Anchoring helps us achieve this.

The concept of anchoring is to think of a positive, biblical thought based on our true identity in Christ—such as "I am blessed, protected, capable and successful." These "I AM" statements are based on who God says we are, and because they come from God, they are powerful for changing us into His image and producing joy and peace inside us! Remember, God is the Great I AM, and He goes before us. When we use the words I AM, make sure to anchor and identify yourself to Him and to use only the words that confirm who God says you are! Everything good comes from Him and because of this, we desire to give Him all the credit and glory for who He has created us to be.

When stating your I AM statements, use your five senses to anchor your true identity with a fragrant essential oil of your choice. There are so many essential oils to choose from. The sense of smell will anchor into your mind the positive words from God, creating a beautiful and positive narration for yourself. Every time we smell that scent in the future, we will be reminded of who we are in Christ, rooting us further into His likeness.

Once you have chosen a scent you like, place the oil in the palm of your hand and press there. Think of Christ and how He was crucified for your healing and wholeness, how He loves you and cares for you. Because Christ lives in us, practicing this simple exercise will help us to remember that God lives within us and is ever present as we touch our palms and remember His touch is in our lives.

As you develop this daily habit of anchoring yourself in Christ using all of your senses, the more automatic it will be for you to think of yourself as blessed, protected, capable and successful. Anchoring can be done anytime, anywhere. Touch the palm of your hand and remember who you are in Christ. You don't need oil, or even touch for that matter, but these senses are from God and are a blessing to us.

We practice anchoring this way because according to the Bible, our true God-given identity is what keeps us grounded and rooted into His truth, which is what helps us to grow and bear fruit. So, we use our true identity as given to us by God to anchor ourselves in Christ. This gives us a sense of peace and strength as we move toward new goals, and it helps us to better receive God's blessings.

This technique can also be very effective when you are facing change or something that is out of your comfort zone. Godly anchoring helps us to feel calm and to make good choices. This reduces self-sabotage and promotes positive change in our lives and helps us to accomplish our goals.

What the Act of Anchoring Looks Like

Some people have never experienced a state of personal power or the feelings of confidence. But through godly meditation, using I AM statements, and godly anchoring, we can begin to experience these things. As we imagine ourselves as constantly anchored in Christ, we can visualize, listen and feel in the clearest detail how different our lives can be when we know Christ is with us.

I recommend that you use the same essential oil each day (a scent you really love), which creates a consistent trigger of good thoughts in your life. Place the oil in the palm of your hand, remembering Jesus Christ and all He has done for you. Smell the oil, and then speak out loud a prayer of thanks to the Lord. Then, begin to state your true identity in Him and the thoughts, feeling and characteristics you wish to have.

During this process, you will use I AM statements that are based in truths from God's Word. You can use the lists in the Appendix to create I AM statements of your own that work for you. For example, if you are struggling with feeling loved, you can pick a scent you like (such as lavender), place it in your palms, smell the lavender, smile and say out loud, "I AM so loved by God. I am precious in His sight. He protects me and cares for me and meets all my needs, because He loves me so very much."

During this process, I encourage you also to visualize the cross and remember the relationship you have with the Lord. Visualize yourself as a clear vessel with God pouring into your life all the words of life that He has for you. Visualize whatever it is you desire to do, such as speaking kindly to your family, forgiving others, speaking at your meeting, conducting yourself with grace…and so on.

Press into the palms of your hands as you continue to visualize all you wish to achieve. Visualize all the details of how you are feeling, looking, standing, moving. Whatever is before you, you will experience it with ease, confidence and strength. Embrace this feeling and visualize yourself with this feeling.

This is an amazing process. By touching your anchor, you are creating a positive trigger to remind you of who you are in Christ. You can activate this godly power anytime and then walk into any situation knowing you will be powerful and strengthened in Christ. (There is an example narration for godly anchoring in the Appendix that you can refer to as you create your own anchoring narration.) You may also include the narration pages you have been working on in your homework.

Resetting Your Mind

At times, you may find yourself needing quick help as you face a sudden situation that arises and triggers you. For example, maybe you unexpectedly encounter someone who has been unkind to you, and suddenly feel fear or anger. Or perhaps you find yourself confronted by a question from a supervisor, and the tone of their voice reminds you of a stressful past experience that makes you feel triggered.

In such situations, you do not have to simply react to the trigger and get caught responding in a way that is not good for you. You can take control, because you are in the driver's seat of your own life. Keep in mind that you cannot hold more than one thought at a time. Take a breath and shift your focus to a positive thought that you would like to have or experience, and anchor this feeling in the palms of your hands. This will help you gain self-control and will give you peace and likely also create a positive outcome in the situation.

If at any time you catch yourself thinking back to the past, or even to a future fear, and you need immediate relief, a great exercise to do is to practice mindfulness. Like a computer, you can learn how to "reboot" yourself. I like to call this technique, "Blink, Blink, What Do I See."

Blink your eyes. Then, blink them again. This act is like a computer reboot. After blinking twice, ask yourself, "What do I see?"

Simply focus on what is around you. What do you see in the room right now? It could be anything—a flower, a green plant, a colorful shirt, someone laughing, a street sign. Just begin naming what you see. As you are naming the things you see, you are bringing your attention to the present, the *now moment*, where God can speak to you. This puts you in position to switch thoughts.

As you do this, your feelings will begin to line up with what you are actually seeing, instead of what you are thinking. Now, name at least one good thing about yourself, perhaps an I AM statement that makes you feel strong, safe, and loved. Now, begin to praise God and thank Him for all that He has given to you.

Use the 5 Keys to Success to Move Forward

Using the 5 Keys to Success (mentioned in Week 1) can also be very helpful in situations like this. For example, I worked with one young woman who had been homeless for several years and had forgotten much of what happened. At times, a memory she had forgotten would suddenly arise, and it would be confusing and upsetting for her.

At such times, I encouraged her to follow the order of the 5 Keys to walk through her thoughts and feelings, so she could put them to rest and find peace. The 5 Keys are effective at helping us to process our experiences.

First, ask yourself what is the **truth**—whatever is true for you and your situation. In her case, her truth was that, in the past she was homeless; it was painful and frightening for her then. But it was several years ago, and the **truth now** is that she has a place to live and is safe.

Next, ask yourself your **goals and purposes.** In this young woman's case, her goal was to be in charge of her life, to own a home, to increase her finances—the purpose of her goals was to be happy and enjoy her life to the fullest. If our goal is to be happy, then we know that going back to our past to pick at the scab of our bad memories is not helpful. We can receive God's grace that things are in our past, and we are protected.

Then, we move on to **planning.** What is our plan to process the memory we're dealing with? It's to use the techniques we have discussed in this book! The plan is to dive right into being aware of our triggers, reprogramming our thoughts, using godly meditation and anchoring, and speaking to ourselves with our new narrator to build ourselves up.

We then take **action** to put those plans to work. We can choose to spend time in God's Word and prayer to encourage ourselves. And we can reach out to our support network to find the encouragement we need as we move forward.

Finally, as we achieve **success** and accomplish our goals, we begin to look for ways to **give back** and help others. Our success grows as we give back to those in need, which is God's desire for us. This gives our life purpose from our past pain, which brings us great joy!

Building on Your New Narration

May these words of my mouth and this meditation of my heart
be pleasing in your sight, Lord, my Rock and my Redeemer.
— **Psalm 19:14 (NIV)**

Now that you have learned some new tools, this is a great time to review your narrations that you have written in previous weeks, as well as the answers to past week's questions. Using the technique of I AM statements and the lists in the Appendix of this book, go to your narration page in this workbook and begin to write down as many positive words that you can think of. Replace every negative word that has run through your mind and any that you find throughout the pages in this workbook. You are forming your new narration, one that is so beautiful and pleasing to God because it in agreement with who He says you are. You will anchor yourself and meditate on these beautiful godly words!

As you do this, remind yourself of the value of repeating these practices religiously as this is going to help you to heal. You are committing to agreeing with God by deciding to take control of your life by taking control of your thoughts! This is a godly practice that will give you great peace!

If you need ideas or inspiration to create a new godly narration that feels right to you, take a look at the sample narrations found in the Appendix. Use them as a guide and personalize your narration to fit you personally.

There Is Always Hope!

I realize these techniques for changing your triggers and reprogramming your mind might seem like a stretch for you at first, maybe even impossible, but remember, this is divine editing and programming—with the emphasis on *divine*. Partner with God and take control of your thoughts and use only the words He would use. Remember, you are powerful! *With God **all** things are possible* (Matthew 19:26 NKJV)—and this includes reprogramming your mind!

Regardless of the circumstances you may be facing right now, I want you to know there is hope. First and foremost, that hope comes from God. He loves you, He is with you, and He wants what is best for you, always! Rely on Him to help you daily as you heal and move forward into a happy life full of success.

Also, be sure to be kind and patient to yourself throughout your daily life. Often, those with PTSD will feel endangered when the situation does not warrant it. Remind yourself often that you are being made new and building a new life.

You are taking control of your life so that you can make choices that benefit you and are pleasing to God. PTSD is not an excuse for bad behavior, but it can often create poor choices until we learn to grow beyond those initial reactions to our negative triggers. God can set you free in every way, as you allow Him to work within your heart and mind.

Having a community of support who offers grace and forgiveness and speaks truth in love is incredibly important to helping you move forward and remain hopeful. And it is vital that the community who supports you is safe and healed.

Remaining connected to a local church is crucial to receiving support, encouragement, spiritual wisdom and healing. Personal time with God through prayer and reading His Word is also important for both the sufferer of PTSD and his or her family. Self-care and doing things that are relaxing and refreshing are also valuable and empowering. PTSD often feels as if it overtakes one's life. Doing things that are enjoyable and life-giving is just as important as confronting the PTSD head-on.

I want you to know that you are going to get better, that you are strong and able to reprogram your negative triggers into positive ones so that you can live a very happy life and have the peace you desire! This is going to be a reality for you! Honor your own worth and awareness and do what is right for you. If you are feeling overwhelmed, reach out to trusted people to get help.

A Prayer for You

Lord, I thank You that according to Your Word, you are transforming me more and more into Your image as I renew my mind. Help me to continue to recognize negative triggers that are causing me to fall into patterns that hold me back, and to reprogram them into positive triggers that glorify You. Help me to constantly think of and practice the Godly Anchoring Tool and I AM statements that build me up and bring me hope. As I divinely edit my thoughts and focus on Your truth, I trust You to put me on the path to accomplishing my goals. Help me to heal completely so I can have a sound mind and a happy life, as you intend for me to have. In Jesus' name, amen.

Week 5: Changing Your Mindset

DAILY HEALING ACTIVITIES

Reminder: Write any positive words from these activities in your new godly narration for this week.

Day 1: Spirituality

Memorize this scripture:

Do not conform to the pattern of this world, but be transformed by the renewing of your mind. Then you will be able to test and approve what God's will is—his good, pleasing and perfect will.
— **Romans 12:2 (NIV)**

Questions to help guide you:

1. What is currently a negative spiritual trigger for you? (Ex. Attending a certain church where you had a past traumatic experience, certain Christian denominations, other spiritual practices, the use of spiritual language to belittle or shame, perhaps even God Himself because you are angry at Him)

　

　

　

2. What positive thing can you associate with your negative spiritual trigger? (Ex. Friendly and kind people who are associated with church, with certain Christian denominations, or other spiritual practices, kind prayers spoken over you)

3. State 3 new positive triggers that you can use to encourage positive feelings about spirituality. (Ex. Whenever I think of church, I think of Sally and how kind she is to me. Or, When I think of people who talk about God, I know that they are generally protective and kind people. Or, When I think of reading the Bible, I remember God has forgiven me and made me pure in His sight.)

_____

_____

_____

4. State 3 things that fit how you desire to feel in your spirituality. "When I am around people, I feel _____." (Ex. Connected, safe, loved)

_____

_____

_____

Week 5: Changing Your Mindset

Day 2: Relationships

Memorize this scripture:

Finally, brothers and sisters, whatever is true, whatever is noble, whatever is right, whatever is pure, whatever is lovely, whatever is admirable—if anything is excellent or praiseworthy—think about such things.
— **Philippians 4:8 (NIV)**

Questions to help guide you:

1. Are there any specific looks that cause you to feel negatively triggered? (Ex. Beards, blonde hair, dark eyes, dark skin, light skin, etc.)

   _____
   _____
   _____

2. What good people could you positively associate this look with? (Ex., trusted helpers such as firemen, doctors who have helped you, good friends, etc.)

   _____
   _____
   _____

3. State 3 new positive triggers. (Ex. I know many people with beards who are kind and thoughtful.)

   _____
   _____
   _____

4. State 3 things that fit how you desire to feel in your relationships. "When I am around (ex. B\bearded, white, blonde)_____people, I feel (Ex. connected, safe, loved) _____"

   _____
   _____
   _____

Day 3: Emotional Health

Memorize this scripture:

May these words of my mouth and this meditation of my heart be pleasing in your sight, Lord, my Rock and my Redeemer.
— Psalm 19:14 (NIV)

Questions to help guide you:

1. What emotion do you have that causes you to feel triggered? (Ex. sadness, grief, fear, caution)

2. What positive trigger could you give to that emotion? (Ex. Wise, grateful, trusting)

3. State 3 new positive triggers. (Ex. Whenever I feel fear, I think of the Lord and how He is always with me and protecting me. When I feel sadness, I think of Jesus and how He wipes away every tear and brings me comfort.)

4. State 3 things that fit how you desire to feel in your emotions. "When I am in touch with my emotions, I feel _____." (Ex. Empowered, content, peaceful)

Week 5: Changing Your Mindset

Day 4: Physical Health

Memorize this scripture:

The Spirit of the Lord is on me, because he has anointed me to proclaim good news to the poor. He has sent me to proclaim freedom for the prisoners and recovery of sight for the blind, to set the oppressed free, to proclaim the year of the Lord's favor.
— Luke 4:18–19 (NIV)

Questions to help guide you:

1. What physically causes you to feel negatively triggered? (Ex. Beauty, weight, nausea, headache, running, walking)

2. What positive trigger could you associate with it? (wellness, self-care, joy, aware)

3. State 3 new positive triggers (Ex. When I am out running, I feel safe and free. When I feel nauseous, I question what I ate that made me not feel well. I am beautiful, safe and valued.)

4. State 3 things that fit how you desire to take care of your physical body. "When I am using my body properly, I feel _____." (Ex. Strong, healthy, alive)

Day 5: Financial Health

Memorize this scripture:

Oh, how I love your law! I meditate on it all day long.
— **Psalm 119:97 (NIV)**

Questions to help guide you:

1. What triggers you negatively about finances? (Ex. Wealthy people—you may think they are abusive. Negative language—your abuser may have told you that you would never be successful.)

2. What positive triggers would you like to create? (ex. Positive words about finances, peace about your bank account)

3. State 3 new positive triggers. (Ex. When I think of wealthy people, I know that I am just as capable of creating wealth as them. There are many wealthy people who are nice and trustworthy. I am created to be successful.)

4. State 3 things that fit how you desire to feel about finances. "When I think of money, I feel _____." (Ex. In control, successful, strong)

Week 5: Changing Your Mindset

Day 6: Career and Serving Others

Memorize this scripture:

My mouth will speak words of wisdom; the meditation of my heart will give you understanding.
— **Psalm 49:3 (NIV)**

Questions to help guide you:

1. What negative trigger do you associate with work or careers? (Ex. Overworked—maybe your abuser forced you to work and all work has become associated with abuse. Controlled—you may have been told what to do.)

2. What positive trigger could you associate with work? (Ex. You enjoy your work and feel productive.)

3. State 3 new positive triggers for work. (Ex. I feel productive and creative when I am working. I know I can gain the skills to do what I want in my career. I am free to choose what I want to do for work.)

4. State 3 things that fit how you desire to feel about career and serving others. "When I am working or serving others, I feel_____." (Ex. Purposeful, energized, intelligent)

Day 7: Sabbath Rest

Memorize this scripture:

May my meditation be pleasing to him, as I rejoice in the Lord.
— Psalm 104:34 (NIV)

Do something to relax and restore yourself today!

Some suggestions for self-care this week include:

- Buy yourself a scented perfume, body wash, candle or essential oil that you can enjoy as you meditate, read the Bible or work on this week's activities.

- Create a vision or inspiration board with photos of places and things that make you happy.

- Enjoy some time with your pet, by taking a walk or playing with your pet.

- Take a long, refreshing bath or shower.

Week 5: Changing Your Mindset

Week 5: Inner Narration

Using what you have learned from this chapter, the scriptures you have memorized this week, and what you discovered while answering this week's questions, build on your original narration from earlier weeks and write an additional short godly narration using only positive words.

Example: I am pleasing to God. I am wise. I am courageous.
I am filled with peace and confidence…etc.

_____

_____

_____

_____

_____

_____

_____

_____

_____

_____

_____

_____

_____

Week 6
Loving Yourself — Body, Mind & Spirit

We love because he first loved us.
— 1 John 4:19 (NIV)

> *Tony was addicted to the high he felt when he was using drugs. He could escape the world, the thoughts that plagued him. For him, it felt as if life stopped for a little while, like he was caring for himself because he needed a break. At least, that was what he told himself, until he was completely unable to manage life at all. He lost everything, including his home and his precious son. Feeling hopeless with nowhere to turn, he went to a local rescue mission. There, he began from the bottom up to build his life, to learn what it meant to truly care for himself. To face the reality of what has happened in his life, including the sexual abuse by his uncle. He had loved his uncle when he was a little boy and felt very confused when the abuse began when he was 10. He really had no one to tell as his mom was single, too busy for him, and he had no idea where his dad was. Feeling trapped, afraid and not knowing what to do because he was so young and innocent, he did nothing and told no one. There were so many things he had to learn as a grown man at the rescue mission.*

Have you ever felt like Tony? If you're saying yes, you're not alone. At times, we all have to figure out the best ways to care for ourselves. Those of us who have faced situations similar to Tony's situation often have to learn as adults what it means to take care of our own well-being, because we didn't learn it from those who should have cared for us and taught us this valuable skill.

The good news is that there is hope! Now, we are adults and we are beginning the process of learning to love and care for ourselves as God does. And God is here to help us every step of the way as we heal and grow in this endeavor. *"Fear not, for I am with you; be not dismayed, for I am your God; I will strengthen you, I will help you, I will uphold you with my righteous right hand.* (Isaiah 41:10 ESV). With His empowerment, grace and strength, we can learn, as Tony did, to care for ourselves well and live in ways that are healthy for us, so that we can enjoy a sound mind and a happy life that is filled with purpose and success.

What Is Self-Care?

Simply put, self-care is the practice of doing things daily that support and strengthen our well-being in body, mind and spirit. It is the practice of caring for the six areas of life — spirituality, relationships, physical wellness, emotional wellness, finances, and career/service. Positive daily activities and habits that keep us healthy in all these areas are essential to our overall well-being, which leads to balance, a sound mind and a happy life, and success.

For those who have suffered abuse, trauma, and dysfunctional childhoods, it can often be a challenge to practice proper, healthy, restorative self-care. We may not even know what it means to care for ourselves. Like Tony, we may have to learn much about how to tend to the needs of our body, mind and spirit in every area of life.

Begin with Learning to Love Oneself

Self-care begins with our ability to love ourselves as God loves us. So, let's take a look at what it means to love ourselves. Loving ourselves is so important! It is the foundation for our healing and our success in life.

I want you to know that you have permission to love yourself. It is not selfish to do so. In fact, properly respecting ourselves and caring about ourselves is something that God desires us to do. We are to see ourselves as God sees us—loved, valuable, fearfully and wonderfully made, and pleasing in His sight!

For many of us, the very idea of loving ourselves may seem foreign and even impossible. We may have learned to be extremely empathetic to others—and yet we can fail to be empathetic to ourselves. Abuse and trauma can lead us to feel guilty for saying no to someone else. We may feel that by not being always available, always giving, we are letting others down. We may have been taught that we are unlovable. Yet if we don't properly care for our own well-being and value ourselves, we won't have the energy and resources we need to care for others or to live a successful life.

Learning to care for ourselves is an act of loving ourselves as God loves us. It takes practice and time, but it is worth it! You are so valuable to God! He wants you to love yourself! He wants you to appreciate all the wonderfulness of who you are in His eyes.

It is important that we learn and put into practice this valuable skill of loving ourselves through self-care, for without properly caring for ourselves, so many struggles can arise in our lives that God has not intended for us to deal with. When we fail to care for ourselves, it can wear us down. We can become exhausted trying too hard to meet the needs of everyone around us except ourselves. We often grow sick, discouraged, and burned out. Our mood, our emotions, our energy levels, our ability to eat well and sleep well can all be impeded, even affecting our faith and our ability to pursue our God-given purpose.

On the other hand, when we know how to set proper boundaries, avoid toxic people, and watch over our own well-being, we can enjoy our lives more. We can engage in habits that are good for us. We can find more joy in our everyday activities, and we can better achieve our goals and purposes.

Let's look at how Tony learned to practice good self-care, and how you can do the same.

Caring for Our Spirit

Tony had to first care for his poor, damaged spirit. He had to do the tough work of forgiving his abuser. And he also had to forgive himself, as he had expressed that he felt like a coward who did nothing to confront his uncle, find help, or make his own life better and safer. Even though he was a boy, he felt anger and guilt over what had happened, and he needed healing from his negative beliefs about himself. He also had to learn of the impact his abuse had on his relationship with God and every area of his life.

As Tony discovered that he was deeply loved by God, he also allowed this love to be his first step toward healing his life. Allowing God's love to heal the wounds in all of our lives is our most important step toward self-care. It is something we need to do every day for ourselves, as His love teaches us how to love ourselves and others.

Tony realized that his spiritual self-care needed to become a daily habit. So, he set aside the needed time first thing in the morning to simply sit quietly and receive God's love. With some helpful direction from the staff at the rescue mission, he started reading God's Word. Because the Bible as a whole felt overwhelming to him, he began with a list of scriptures given to him that focused on God's love. These scriptures can be found in the daily activities in each chapter of this book, the ones you have been memorizing weekly. As you let these scriptures become real and powerful to you, they will transform how you see yourself and God, just as they did for Tony.

Caring for Our Mind

As he cared for his spiritual well-being, Tony simultaneously began cleansing his mind, creating a new narration for himself that would bring healing. He was very intentional about leaving notes around his room with questions like, "Do you want to be well?" He knew he had to get his mind right, to where it no longer tormented him with thoughts of failure or tempted him with thoughts to use and abuse his body, both with drugs and sex.

Again, with the help of a facilitator who encouraged him to follow godly principles of self-care, Tony began writing a new narration with words that he has longed to hear his whole life: "I AM a son of the King. I AM loved. I AM cared for and cherished. I AM forgiven and free!" The list was quite long, and he continually added to it as words came to mind about what he wanted to hear and feel. (Tony's narration is provided for you in the Appendix.) As he continued to meditate on these words and encourage himself with them, he learned to treat himself as a loving father would treat him if he had one here in this life.

His inner voice began to mirror and speak the loving, kind, positive, helpful words that God would say to him. He began to believe God's words deep in his soul. He additionally used this list as a way to affirm himself throughout the day. Whenever he wanted to feel encouraged and good about himself, he would say, "I am strong, I am loved, I am courageous…" As he learned this new way of speaking, he began to only say the words that he knew God would say to him. He learned that God is the great I AM, and he began to understand that God goes before him. So, when he used I AM statements, he began to feel so much more connected to God, and felt the Lord's strength rising within him as he went about his daily life.

Tony began to value education and wanted to improve his mind by learning a skill that would allow him to hold a great job. He studied computer science and graduated with a degree in IT. He will be graduating from the mission with a job at California Behavioral Health.

Caring for Our Body

As Tony learned that the body, mind and spirit are all connected, he knew it was important to care for his body—not only by keeping it free from alcohol, sex and drugs, but also making good choices about the foods he put into his body and the exercise he would need each day to stay mentally and physically strong.

Rest and relaxation were difficult for Tony to learn at first, as these things were very unfamiliar to him. He had to literally force himself to sit and read a book for pleasure or take a restful nap or a peaceful walk. To help support his new self-care habits, Tony chose to make himself a schedule and followed it closely. He scheduled one day off a week to simply do whatever activities he pleased that were within the healthy choices given to him. This daily schedule empowered him to make good choices, which helped him to build his ability to take good care of his own needs in positive ways.

Great Results Happen When We Practice Good Self-Care

It has been almost two years for Tony now at the rescue mission. And it has been a wonderful journey of healing for him. He has received custody of his son, who is now living with him at the mission. Tony and his son are enjoying a happy life!

Tony is an example of receiving healing through loving oneself body, mind and spirit.

You, too, are going to do great things because you have chosen to heal, and to love yourself.

The habits that you establish for yourself will help you to receive love, to reprogram your mind and to care for your body!

Always remember this: Your life is significant. It has purpose and meaning. God has designed you to do great things. He has great plans for you. His grace is present in our lives to help us accomplish it all, but we have a role to play as well in having a successful future filled with godly purpose. There are things we can do to shape our future. It is not that we need to do anything to win the Lord's approval. In Christ, we are already loved, accepted, and welcome to be in His presence. We are not earning anything from Him; He has already given us all we need through His grace.

But there are actions we need to take daily to put things in motion in our lives. It's like growing flowers or fruit. First, we must plant a seed. And then we care for that seed with water, sunlight, and fertilizer. Then the seed grows. The flower and fruit come from the creative power that God has placed in the seed. Our part is to put the seed in the ground and then care for it. It is similar with our future. He has a purpose for us, and as we plant the seeds and habitually care for them, God will provide the creative power, the blessings, and the increase to produce the results we desire to see.

So, how do we know what seeds to plant? What actions to take for our future? We take time to position ourselves to hear from God. And self-care is a vital part of the process!

As Tony discovered, and as you will discover too, when you get quiet during times of self-care, that is when God can speak to you. He can and certainly does speak to you throughout the busyness of the day, but when you get quiet and rest, He can restore you and give you all that you will need to accomplish the great plans He has for you. The more you come to know the Lord, the more you will come to know yourself and greatly realize the purpose He has given you to accomplish.

Creating Our Daily Self-Care Habits for Success

An essential element to building our self-care routine is to establish daily activities that encourage us to take care of our lives and stay balanced. We do this through *our habits*. What are habits? They are a practice we undertake regularly.

For many of us, we may have learned to develop any number of unhealthy habits and negative coping skills. You may recognize some of these unhealthy habits in your own life, because at the time, they were the only way you could deal with the abuse or trauma you faced. These unhealthy coping skills may include things such as self-medication, binge eating, alcohol and drug use, excessive sleep, uncontrollable anger, defensiveness, an addiction to gaining the approval of other people, trusting everyone, trusting no one, holding grudges, disassociation, denial, passive-aggression, rationalizations, and other negative ways of thinking and behaving.

As you have probably discovered at some point, these unhealthy ways of approaching life do not produce good results in your life. Instead, they hinder you from reaching your goals. They don't add to your happiness, but instead tend to take away from it. It's important to recognize what is not working well for you, and to make changes that allow you to better care for yourself in ways that are positive, so that you can have a joyful, successful life.

We do this through exchanging unhealthy coping skills for healthy habits. What is a healthy habit? It is anything we do that produces good fruits and benefits in our lives and is in alignment with God's Word, The Bible. A healthy habit will produce a well-balanced, joyful, and purposeful life.

As you practice healthy habits, you'll discover something amazing: it *feels good* to take care of yourself and to love yourself. Self-care increases our confidence and our enjoyment of everyday life. Think about activities that make you feel confident, happy, content and at peace. Even simple acts such as grooming yourself, doing your nails, brushing your hair, or giving yourself a neck rub are positive messages that indicate you care about your well-being and want to look and feel your best, which builds your self-esteem.

Other actions that we may consider as positive, healthy habits might include enjoying a cup of tea, taking a nap when you are tired, going for a walk in a park you like, reading, deep breathing, meditating on God's Word, or talking on the phone with a good friend who cares about your well-being. All the things you do that add benefits to your life can fit into the category of healthy habits and healthy coping skills, as they lead you towards a better future.

Our daily habits are crucial because, no matter how big or small they may seem, they define us. Our habits make us who we are. What we do each and every day determines what our future will become. As we choose to practice healthy self-care, it becomes easier for us to consistently make use of positive activities that build us up and bring about good results.

With all this said, I want to encourage you to be patient with yourself as you begin to heal and develop positive habits of self-care. Habits are not intended to overwhelm you, but instead to make you more productive and feel good about yourself.

Spiritual Habits

As we learn to love ourselves, it also becomes easier to receive the love of God for us. And as we learn to receive the love of God, it becomes easier to love ourselves. Meditating on God's love for us brings true transformation and healing, so that we can have the joyful life He desires us to have. For this reason, developing healthy spiritual habits is the essential foundation for finding balance and well-being in every area of life.

The habits that help us develop our spiritual connection with God include daily prayer, reading His Word, meditating on His promises and love, worship, praise, thankfulness, and time spent with those of similar faith, such as in a Bible study or church group. These spiritual activities help us to build our relationship with Jesus, who is our center, our source, the vital heart of everything we do as Christians. Through our daily spiritual habits, we will also know and understand His words so that they help guide and direct us in our daily choices, which leads to our success.

Just as with any relationship, the more we nurture our relationship with God the more connected we feel towards Him and the more like Him we become. Our character reflects His as we develop more peace, more power, more love, more forgiveness and even more self-care. Jesus took time to be alone and to care for Himself, and He desires this for you as well.

Relationship Habits

Our most important relationships will always be our relationship with God and our relationship with ourselves. As we grow in these areas and tend to ourselves and to our spirituality, we will be more empowered to build positive, healthy relationships with those around us—our spouse, our children, our family, our friends, and our coworkers. And there are many things we can do daily to help all our connections be uplifting, encouraging, and strong.

For example, we can offer daily affirmations to the people in our life that we are close to. The more we affirm them regularly, the more loved they will feel, which is good for them and for us.

We then get that love and affirmation back, and it helps us to feel better about ourselves and our relationships. When we serve others, they feel loved. When we are aware of our boundaries, we can be kind to others and exhibit self-care. This giving and receiving is to be a continual cycle that brings about benefits for us and those we are connected to.

Emotional Habits

Remember what we have discussed in previous chapters: every part of our lives impacts our well-being in other areas. This is so true for our emotional wellness. When we take proper care of our emotions, we'll be better able to make good choices for our physical health, relationships, career, and so on. And when we take care of those areas, we'll feel better emotionally. Everything overlaps, and we can use that to our advantage!

One way to take care of our emotional health is to develop habits that help us maintain balance in our emotional lives. This includes doing little things daily that we enjoy, such as going for a walk, caring for our pets, eating a healthy meal, and meditating on our new narrations. Setting aside time daily to anchor ourselves as discussed in chapter 5 is very helpful to our emotional well-being, as is saying our positive I AM affirmations each day. Make it a habit to speak kindly to yourself as much as possible. All of these things will help you to stay balanced, feel good, and be uplifted.

Physical Habits

Our physical habits are essential to helping us take care of our bodies. A lot of times, we can get so caught up in our head that we can lose sight of our care for our body. So, it can be very helpful to make conscious, mindful choices about how we will tend to our physical wellness. Creating a daily schedule can be very helpful for fitting in appointments with ourselves to do something healthy for our bodies.

For example, you might make it a daily habit to get up early and take a walk in the fresh air and sunshine. This is healthy because as you move your body, your muscles get strengthened and you feel good. It's also really good for your mood. Eating well is another habit that is very good for your body, as we tend to feel healthier and happier when we are choosing foods that nourish our bodies. Additionally, getting plenty of water every day is really healthy, helping us to stay hydrated, refreshed, and alert.

Another thing I've found to be helpful is to spend time on physical grooming and self-care when I need a little extra tender-loving care. If you're feeling tired or need a pick-me-up, a relaxing bath with lit candles and good music can feel wonderful for your body and your mind. Getting a massage, taking a swim in a pool, or enjoying a good shower can feel wonderful and put you in a good mood.

Financial Habits

Finances can be very stressful for many people, and much of that stress can be turned around as we develop positive financial habits. After all, no one wants to feel stressed about money and bills. It is a good thing for our emotions, our physical well-being, and our careers when we learn to take good care of our finances.

The financial habits you begin to develop often start with how you think and speak to yourself about money. Many of us have learned to tell ourselves what is negative, such as, "I'll never have enough money," or, "I'm just not good with a budget." To create better financial habits, it's important to speak positive things over yourself, even if you do not yet make money. Make it a daily habit to use positive I AM statements about your finances, such as "I am able to manage my budget. I am trusting God to help me make good financial decisions."

Proper financial self-care is a skill that can be developed. Take a class in person or online. Learn from others who are skilled in managing their money. The more you know about finances, the better you will feel as you gain control over the money in your life. God has said those who are faithful with little will be faithful with much (Luke 16:10), and He will continue to pour financial blessings into your life as you continue to be faithful in your habits toward money.

As you break past negative habits and choose good ones, such as spending responsibly, trusting God, and showing confidence that you can handle finances, it will help you think properly and healthily about money. You will begin to transform and spend your money and save it wisely. This positive way of thinking and behaving, in turn, improves your ability to step into and maintain a good career too—because you will be acting in ways that line up with a belief that you are good with money, which includes having a successful career.

Career and Serving Habits

Developing good habits in the area of work and serving others will set you up for long-term success in whatever you do. Always work as if you are working for the Lord (Colossians 3:23). Even if you're not working right now, you can start to develop good habits by imagining how you will maintain a job when you get one. How will you communicate and build a network with others? Where will your money go when you do get a job? Will you put some of it in savings, buy healthy foods, pay rent, etc.? All of these answers can encourage you to feel inspired for your future and will help you to make good decisions as you pursue a career.

Other habits that are good for you in this area of life include deciding what you would like to do for work (or volunteering), and then developing the skills to be a success. Perhaps you will want to attend classes at a local community college to develop the skills to be a nurse. Perhaps you can practice using a computer so that you can become faster at it. Maybe you'll want to spend time daily to work on your resume so you can apply for new jobs.

Habits for Our Sabbath Rest

Keep in mind as well that we are all entitled to some rest throughout the week. Enjoying a Sabbath rest is valuable to restore yourself and relax, so you can be ready to return to your job or other activities refreshed and ready to take on new challenges. On Sundays, for example, you may decide to do whatever it is that restores your energy and enthusiasm. Make it a habit to take time off from all the week's work, recuperate, and plan ahead for the coming week.

Remember, this is a long life and we must take care of ourselves. We must love ourselves as the creation of Christ, as children of the King, worthy of all that is good and pleasing. Love yourself with the same love you would offer to your child whom you love. You are God's child created in His image, and He loves you! Much of the loving and nurturing we do for ourselves has to do with resting in God's love. So, fit a sabbath rest into your weekly schedule and use it to receive God's love for yourself.

A Prayer for You

Father God, I thank You for showing me just how much You love me, and for helping me to grow in the knowledge of Your amazing love for me every day of my life. Thank You for helping me to grow in love for myself and teaching me ways that I can lovingly and attentively take proper care of my needs in the six areas of life. Help me to notice the times when I am not practicing the self-care I need, so I can switch gears and take steps to stay strong and healthy spiritually, in my relationships, emotionally, physically, in my finances, and in my career and my service to others. In Jesus' name, amen.

DAILY HEALING ACTIVITIES

Reminder: Write any positive words from these activities in your new godly narration for this week.

Day 1: Spirituality

Memorize this scripture:

So, God created mankind in his own image, in the image of God he created them; male and female he created them.
— Genesis 1:27 (NIV)

Questions to help guide you:

1. What spiritual practices do you currently have in place? (Ex. I only read my Bible on Sundays right now. I don't really go to church. I like to play praise music when I'm in the shower.)

   _____
   _____
   _____

2. What spiritual habits would you like to begin to do regularly? (Ex, I want to read and memorize one scripture every day. I want to find a weekly Bible study that I enjoy.)

   _____
   _____
   _____

3. State 3 positive things you can do to help yourself practice good spiritual habits successfully. (Ex. I'll get up 15 minutes earlier each day so I can have time to pray. I'll attend a Bible study once a week. I'll thank God for three good things in my life every night before I go to sleep.)

   _____
   _____
   _____

Week 6: Loving Yourself — Body, Mind & Spirit

Day 2: Relationships

Memorize this scripture:

Therefore, if anyone is in Christ, the new creation has come: The old has gone, the new is here!
— 2 Corinthians 5:17 (NIV)

Questions to help guide you:

1. What relationship practices do you currently have in place? (Ex. I spend time daily with my spouse. I don't call my parents as much as I'd like to. I forget to check in on my friend unless I need a favor.)

2. What relationship habits would you like to begin to do regularly? (Ex. I'd like to see my friends once a month for coffee or a nice meal. I'd like to pray each morning for 5-10 minutes with my children. I want to make new friends who lift me up and are encouraging to be around.)

3. State 3 positive things you can do to help yourself practice good relationship habits successfully. (Ex. I can set aside time every Saturday morning to call a friend or relative I want to check in with. I will go places where I can make positive new friends.)

Day 3: Emotional Health

Memorize this scripture:

Certainly, you made my mind and heart; you wove me together in my mother's womb.
— Psalm 139:13 (NET Bible)

Questions to help guide you:

1. What emotional practices do you currently have in place? (Ex. I tend to stuff down unpleasant emotions instead of facing them. I'm not good at recognizing how I feel.)

2. What emotional habits would you like to begin to do regularly? (Ex. I want to meditate daily on things that make me happy. I'd like to listen to more uplifting music.)

3. State 3 positive things you can do to help yourself practice good emotional habits successfully. (Ex. I will get outside daily for at least 10 minutes for my emotional health. I will listen to happy music every day at lunch to refresh myself. I'll take a break daily to have a nice cup of tea and enjoy watching birds outside my window.)

Week 6: Loving Yourself — Body, Mind & Spirit

Day 4: Physical Health

Memorize this scripture:

In peace I will lie down and sleep, for you alone, Lord, make me dwell in safety.
— **Psalm 4:8 (NIV)**

Questions to help guide you:

1. What physical practices do you currently have in place? (Ex. I currently take a walk three times a week. I used to go the gym regularly, but I haven't been in the last two months. I stay up late and then feel tired in the morning.)

2. What physical habits would you like to begin to do regularly? (Ex. I'd like to take a yoga class on Mondays. I want to eat better and feel better physically. I'd like to get 7-8 hours of sleep every day.)

3. State 3 positive things you can do to help yourself practice good physical habits successfully. (Ex. I will eat more salads during the week. I will no longer buy ice cream unless it's a special occasion. I will take a class to help me learn how to use the gym equipment safely.)

Day 5: Financial Health

Memorize this scripture:

Honor the Lord with your wealth, with the firstfruits of all your crops; then your barns will be filled to overflowing, and your vats will brim over with new wine.
–Proverbs 3:9-10 (NIV)

Questions to help guide you:

1. What financial practices do you currently have in place? (Ex. I budget my money weekly. I don't set aside money to put in a savings account. I don't pay tithing.)

   _____
   _____
   _____

2. What financial habits would you like to begin to do regularly? (Ex. I want to set aside 10% of my income for savings. I want to tithe 10% of my income.)

   _____
   _____
   _____

3. State 3 positive things you can do to help yourself practice good financial habits successfully. (Ex. I will take a class or watch a video on how to set up my budget properly and invest my money. I will surround myself with the right people who help me to be responsible, so I do not indulge or overspend. I will dedicate 15 minutes in the evening to review and write down what I have spent for the day.)

   _____
   _____
   _____

Week 6: Loving Yourself — Body, Mind & Spirit

Day 6: Career and Serving Others

Memorize this scripture:

In the same way, let your light shine before others, so that they may see your good works and give glory to your Father who is in heaven.
— Matthew 5:16 (ESV)

Questions to help guide you:

1. What career and serving practices do you currently have in place? (Ex. I have a job, but I don't enjoy it. I work all the time, but I don't get a chance to volunteer in children's church the way I'd like to.)

   _____
   _____
   _____

2. What career and serving habits would you like to begin to do regularly? (Ex. I'd like to find a job that doesn't require me to work on Sundays. I'd like to learn more about how I can volunteer at church. I'd like to study nursing so I can become a nurse.)

   _____
   _____
   _____

3. State 3 positive things you can do to help yourself practice good career and serving habits successfully. (Ex. I can make a new resume so I can start a job search. I can talk to my boss to find out if I can train in a new skill that would be useful in my career. I'll attend the volunteer meeting at church to see what opportunities for volunteering they may have for me.)

   _____
   _____
   _____

Day 7: Sabbath Rest

Memorize this scripture:

I thank you, God, for making me so mysteriously complex! Everything you do is marvelously breathtaking. It simply amazes me to think about it! How thoroughly you know me, Lord!
— **Psalm 139:14 (TPT)**

Do something to relax and restore yourself today! Meditate and think about how much God loves you! Do what brings you joy, that might be bringing someone else flowers today. Spread love and good feelings through smiling and speaking kindly. Take a nap. Go to bed early.

Week 6: Inner Narration

Using what you have learned from this chapter, the scriptures you have memorized this week, and what you discovered while answering this week's questions, build on your original narration from earlier weeks and write an additional short godly narration using only positive words.

Example: I am powerful in the Lord. I am bold. I am filled with His joy. I am able to relax and enjoy times of rest and peace…etc.

Week 7
Putting It All Together

Praise be to the God and Father of our Lord Jesus Christ, the Father of compassion and the God of all comfort, who comforts us in all our troubles, so that we can comfort those in any trouble with the comfort we ourselves receive from God. For just as we share abundantly in the sufferings of Christ, so also our comfort abounds through Christ.
— 2 Corinthians 1:3-5 NIV

Susie could not imagine that there was anything in this life that could take away her pain. Thoughts tortured her every moment of the day! Even her nights were restless, and her dreams were filled with nightmares from the past. Going to therapists and constantly talking of her abuse seemed to go nowhere and only made things worse. Finally, after coming to the local rescue mission and taking the course on Complete Healing, she began to be committed to the very thought of completely healing. Nevertheless, she still had doubts and so many questions. She continued to do her homework and surrendered to the opportunity of allowing God's love to heal her. Even on days when she didn't feel like it, she did her homework; she read and memorized scriptures, and began to visualize and imagine herself helping others. Days were often long for her in the beginning and it felt like slow healing, but she took things one day at a time, and after only seven weeks she couldn't believe her transformation! She now not only knows about Jesus and His love for her, but also experiences this love on a constant basis. Her mind speaks to her with kindness throughout the day, and her nights are filled with peace and deep rest. She feels more equipped and is able to pray for and bless others with the same hope and healing that she has been given. Her purpose of helping others far exceeded any expectation she had of her healing. She never imagined before now that she would feel this happy and well! Now that she is filled with passion and purpose, she can't wait to get up and share her story of redemption with others! She desires for others to experience what she has experienced, complete healing!

As you can see from Susie's story, the process of surrendering and allowing God's love to transform our thinking, our priorities and our life brings complete healing! God is so good! You don't have to remain stuck in the past any longer. You have opened up your life to a new, healthy, godly way of thinking about and caring for yourself. You have chosen to embrace the good life that God has planned for you. Now, you can move forward into the rest of your life with joy, enthusiasm, and hope for good things while carrying out your purpose and caring for others—living a life that is fulfilled in every way!

Take Inventory of Your Life

You may be nearing the end of this book, but you have so much ahead of you. God has great plans for you! *"For I know the plans I have for you," declares the Lord, "plans to prosper you and not to harm you, plans to give you hope and a future"* (Jeremiah 29:11 NIV). Your role is to find ways to live out these plans in ways that are pleasing to God and that bring about blessings for you and for others.

Take a look at where you are at right now. This is a great time to look back at the work you've done in previous weeks and consider how you have changed in just this short amount of time. Have you accomplished some of the goals you set for yourself in weeks 1, 2, 3, 4, 5 and 6? Have you discovered new goals you would like to reach for? Each and every one of us would be wise to set new goals and constantly change and grow into the likeness of Christ.

As you read through your answers to the questions and activities you've done in the past several weeks, you may also realize that there are areas where you have not yet achieved some of your desired goals. There may be more work to do—and this is normal! We are all a work in progress. We never reach perfection in this life, but that doesn't have to stop us from continuing to be more Christlike. Remember, we are always growing in the Lord, as we allow Him to work within us. His desire for every one of us is that *these grace ministries will function until we all attain oneness in the faith, until we all experience the fullness of what it means to know the Son of God, and finally we become one perfect man with the full dimensions of spiritual maturity and fully developed in the abundance of Christ* (Ephesians 4:13 TPT).

This process of assessing yourself is something that you will want to do throughout your life. Continue the practice of re-evaluating where you are in each of the six key areas of life—spirituality, relationships, physical wellness, emotional wellness, finances, and career/service. This will help you to know your needs, remain on track with your goals, and enjoy more and more success.

I encourage you to begin with *weekly* evaluations of how you are doing in these six areas. Perhaps make time to do this on Sunday (or whenever you take your sabbath rest), as a way to honor what you achieved that week and prepare yourself for the week ahead of you. Read your new narration daily, anchor yourself in Christ daily, and focus on who you are in Him continually. Remind yourself of how far you have come and rejoice!

Then, as you make more progress with your goals and find yourself maintaining what you have desired to do for yourself, you might move into a *monthly* evaluation. Whatever schedule works for you, remember to make it a regular practice by adding this time to your calendar. Be honest with yourself and God so that you can continue to experience success, wellness, a sound mind and a happy life.

Remain Aware of Your Needs

The healing process you have gone through in reading this book has been a full one, and you have come such a long way! This is something to be proud of and rejoice over. And it is something to continue to live out for the rest of your life. As you go through your daily activities, remember that it is always valuable and effective to take good care of yourself and your needs.

This is one reason that taking regularly inventory of the six key areas of the circle can be so effective. If you do not take inventory and check to see what your needs are, you run the risk of running empty, being bitter, and burning out. God has a much better way for you than that. As you regularly assess how you're doing, you'll become much more aware of your own needs and be much more able to take care of yourself properly, so that you can also take care of others. Remember, we will have a harder time caring for others if we cannot care for ourselves. Self-care is therefore beneficial to both you and others!

Recognizing what you need in each area of life at any given moment can be eye-opening, and so freeing. Your goal is to remain balanced, which leads you to a sound mind and a happy life. You've worked hard in this course to gain that balance, and now is the time to maintain it.

Ask yourself where you are in each of the six areas. What needs more work in your spiritual life? Your relationship life? Do you need to forgive anyone? If you are upset at someone else's behavior, can you look at yourself and notice yourself acting that way too? Do you need to change your behavior so that you are not hurting others?

As you follow this process of considering each area on a regular basis, you will have a greater sense of what you need and want to do day by day to stay in balance. You'll recognize areas where you need to grow.

And it is a useful way to stay in touch with what you can do to take care of your own needs daily. You'll find it easier to recognize when, for example, it would be helpful for you to stretch and go take a walk outside (a need for physical self-care), or perhaps to take a long, soaking bath in lavender Epsom salts (a need for emotional self-care), or to call a friend and hear a kind voice (emotional and relationship self-care). When you recognize such needs, you can then act on them, giving yourself the love and support you deserve.

As you stay aware of your own needs and meet them in appropriate, healthy ways, your overall well-being will grow and remain strong. You'll find it easier to maintain a sound mind and a sense of joy. And you'll be better positioned for what God has called you to do in your life. As you care for yourself, you will know how to care for others and your purpose will begin to grow, and you will become even more fulfilled! It is a win-win all around!

Take Note of the Needs of Others

Have you ever noticed an elderly person struggling to get their groceries into or out of their car? Did you feel a tug on your heart, a desire to help them carry their bags so they didn't have to struggle alone? Perhaps you have seen stray cats and dogs in your neighborhood and wished you could help care for them. Or maybe you have seen a friend struggle with their health and considered helping them by offering to exercise with them or share healthy recipes.

We are all called to make a difference in the lives of others. The drive and desire to help other people is something that God has put within each of us, and we can feel that need when we allow ourselves to be aware of it. If you are noticing that others around you have needs, and you feel a desire to help them, then you are simply tapping into what God has put within you. And this is a great blessing for you—and for those you will help!

One of the greatest gifts God gives to us is the ability to reach out to others in His name. You have a purpose in life that goes beyond just living. You are chosen by God to bless others, to make a difference in the lives of those around you. When you respond to this godly desire to help others, and follow through, it feels right and good. As you continue to develop yourself in the Lord and receive His comfort, you will have an even greater desire to comfort and respond with help to others, further increasing your joy and fulfillment.

As someone who has experienced abuse and gained healing in my own life, I find my greatest joy in comforting others and helping them to find their healing and come to know the Lord. You, too, can take your painful past and what you have learned and use it to bless others who have gone through similar situations. It may be that you'll help someone who went through something similar as you. It may be that you'll meet people who need to learn a skill such as self-care that you now know about and can share with them. The ways you can bring aid to others is numerous, full of variety and opportunity.

There are so many people who need our help in life. We all have a role to play in reaching others with God's goodness!

Positioning Yourself to Be a Blessing

To be as effective as you can be at bringing good things into the lives of others, we first need to be filled up with the love of God. We must receive His energy and empowerment so that we can do our part to bless others as He has called us to do. *Do not neglect to do good and to share what you have, for such sacrifices are pleasing to God* (Hebrews 13:16 ESV).

It will be hard to point others to Jesus if you yourself are not following Him. Therefore, one vital way to be ready to do good is to spend time daily with the Lord, taking in the strength, guidance, and joy that He wants to share with you. Take what you have learned in this book, stay focused on the scriptures we have shared here in addition to learning more of the Bible and other great books. Talk with God daily about what He would have you do with your life.

Remember, too, that you do not have to be perfect before you help others. You can continue to grow in your own healing while you serve the needs of those around you. Simply take what you have learned and bless others with this knowledge. A smile, a kind word, and a gentle prayer when others need it can be so effective at meeting someone where they are at. The tools you have practiced — such as I AM statements, self-care tips, anchoring yourself, and creating a new narration — are all skills you can share with others who would benefit from them.

Using the 5 Keys to Success to Set Future Goals

As you grow in your personal life and your service to others, you will discover that your goals will grow and change too. For this reason, it is useful to continue to apply the 5 Keys to Success in each area of your life. Let's take a look at these 5 keys again, in light of everything you have learned in previous weeks.

Key 1: Truth

God said you shall know the truth, and the truth will set you free (John 8:32). Truth is like putting a dot on the map so you will know where you are. In week one, you learned to discover the truth about your past, the abuse you experienced, and its impact on your life. Now, you will continue to seek and discover the truth as you grow and experience new things in life.

There is a constant truth that never changes, like the Bible, and then there is the truth about us. How have we changed? Where do we need more work? Truth is critical for success in every area of our life. We must know what we are to change in order to set and attain new goals. As you move forward in life, regularly return to the use of this key to assess where you are at and what you want to change. Beginning with spirituality, ask yourself honestly what the truth is about your current circumstances. Then, move on to asking the same question for all the other areas of life. This sets you up to begin to move from where you are right now to where you'd like to be.

Key 2: Goals and Their Purpose

Setting new goals continually keeps us growing. Remember, there is always a purpose behind each goal. In Week 2, you set goals to help you move forward in healing, such as spending time in God's Word so you can learn how loved you are in Christ. Setting goals such as these helps us to accomplish the purposes God has for our life, making us more effective in all that we do. Purpose is the bigger picture, and it is what will give energy to our goal. Without purpose, we are lost in the world, just consuming oxygen and waiting for it all to end. When we lose our purpose, our energy becomes depleted as the zest for "what could have been" slowly begins to fade away.

As you move forward in life, continue to evaluate your goals and remind yourself of their purpose. Notice the times that things are going well, and also the times you are feeling burned out or not as passionate about your goals. If you are finding yourself disheartened, disappointed, and drained from the hours in the day, then it is quite possible that you have forgotten your purpose. Allow God to re-instill in you the purpose behind each one of your goals so that great joy and energy will return and encourage you to keep moving forward, to grow and to become more of who you are meant to be.

Key 3: Plan

Dreams and their purposes need planning. Once the light bulb has gone on and your energy and excitement has returned, the next step is creating a plan for how you will accomplish your goals and achieve their purposes. In Week 3, we learned that planning is much like deciding you will travel somewhere (the goal), and then writing down directions or highlighting the roads on a map (your plan) so you can begin to head toward your destination. Through the activities in this book, you have made plans that have helped you moved forward in your healing, such as getting up early to spend 15 minutes reading the Bible every day. And you will continue to set plans as you move through life.

Gather with healthy people who will help you to set realistic plans for your goals. Pray about your plans and allow God to show you in detail with great clarity what your next steps are. He will not give you an overburdening plan. It will be realistic and obtainable. God tells us He knows the plans He has for us (Jeremiah 29:11), so ask Him! This will help you to move toward your goal with purpose effectively, because you will know where you are going!

Key 4: Action

Without action, truth, purpose and planning are nothing more than wasted information. The good news is that once you have established what is truth, set your goal, found its purpose and devised the plan, action is easy! In weeks 4, 5 and 6, you were encouraged to choose actions that would help you stick to your plans and accomplish your goals and purposes, such as creating safe spaces, setting better boundaries, and connecting with safe, healthy people who can help you stay on track toward success.

With all the newfound energy and excitement that you will gain from taking good actions, going about each day will be a joy! Make sure to surround yourself with people who will hold you accountable and share in your excitement and joy as you move forward! With proper follow through, your goals can become reality. Hold to your healing and success and make it happen!

Key 5: Rewards

When you practice the first four keys, you will be rewarded with success! This is the point where the keys then must be repeated, which is what we are talking about here in week 7. At this stage, we celebrate our accomplishments, which we achieved by following the 5 Keys! You can celebrate how far you have come since beginning this book, rejoicing in the healing and success you have already begun to experience because God is faithful and you have chosen to follow through with the goals, plans and actions you have set in earlier weeks. Now, you can expect the rewards from the first four keys to begin pouring into your life!

As you become successful and reach your goals, your question then becomes, "What is the truth of why I have been blessed? What now is my purpose for this success? Who will I help? What plan of action will I take to bless others?" Doing this ensures even more success for you as the cycle gets repeated in the lives of others. You will gain even more happiness, joy and fulfillment as all the keys have been given to you. And as you pass on your success to help others, it perpetuates even more success in your life too.

Your Future, Purpose and Legacy

How do you know what your life will be like tomorrow?
Your life is like the morning fog-it's here a little while, then it's gone.
— **James 4:14 (NLT)**

Our lives pass quickly! Although some days may seem long, this life can be and is very short, especially in comparison to the eternity we will one day live with the Lord. We are like a vapor that can fade away at any moment.

We don't know when our time will come, which means it is important to make the most of what we are given each day. We need to be careful how we live. Our lives must be intentional and filled with purpose so that we can leave a positive impact on those we come in contact with in our lives.

People watch us, and we are either an influence for good, or for bad. What is exciting is that we get to choose! Let us choose each day to leave a lasting legacy for good, to be known as children of the King, followers of Jesus Christ, emulating Him and drawing others to Him so their lives can be impacted for good! As we live for the Lord, mindful of our legacy, we will find ourselves paying attention to what we say and do, and the seeds we plant into the lives of other people.

What do you see for your future? What is your purpose? What do you want to be known for? There will be many opportunities over your lifetime to gain new successes and accomplish new goals. Your life will change, you will change, people and circumstances will change, so it is important to continually look at the truth in each area, create a new goal, find the purpose in it, plan for it, have someone hold you accountable for it, and when you reap the success, give back!

I encourage you to consider all the ways in which God may be calling you to leave a lasting legacy. And if you would like to help others the way this book has helped you, consider becoming a coach for Christ! You have learned so many skills in this book that can help others. By learning to coach others, you can add such value to them as they receive the healing they need as well, so they, too, can have a sound mind and a happy life, and leave a legacy for the Lord.

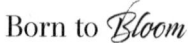

A Prayer for You

Lord, I thank You for all that I have learned and gained in these past several weeks as I have read this book. You are so good! Thank You for working in my life, bringing about my healing, and showing me how to have the abundant life You have promised! Lord, I ask You to give me insights into what my future holds. Help me to know Your purpose for me, and all You have for me. Help me to be a blessing to others and to lead them to You. In Jesus' name, amen.

Week 7: Putting It All Together

DAILY HEALING ACTIVITIES

Reminder: Write any positive words from these activities in your new godly narration for this week.

Day 1: Spirituality

Memorize this scripture:

Choose a good reputation over great riches; being held in high esteem is better than silver or gold.
— Proverbs 22:1 (NLT)

Questions to help guide you:

1. How do you want to be remembered for your spirituality? List three ways you want to leave an impact on the world with your spirituality. (Ex. I want to be remembered as a true follower of Christ by (1) my obedience, (2) my hospitality to others, (3) my generosity.)

2. What are three things you can do to help achieve your three goals mentioned above? (Ex. I can offer to pray for others when they're in need. I can offer to serve a friend a meal at my home. I can give $5 a month to support a local soup kitchen.)

Day 2: Relationships

Memorize this scripture:

But the love of the Lord remains forever with those who fear him. His salvation extends to the children's children of those who are faithful to his covenant, of those who obey his commandments!
— Psalm 103:17 (NLT)

Questions to help guide you:

1. How do you want to be remembered in your relationships? List three ways you want to leave an impact on others in the area of relationships. (Ex. I want to be remembered by my family for (1) being available to them, (2) showing and teaching them about Jesus, and (3) my service toward them.)

2. What are three things you can do to help achieve your three goals mentioned above? (Ex. I can make sure to attend my son's sports games. I can read a scripture each day with my family at dinner. I can wash their laundry as unto the Lord.)

Week 7: Putting It All Together

Day 3: Emotional Health

Memorize this scripture:

Let each generation tell its children of your mighty acts; let them proclaim your power.
— **Psalm 145:4 (NLT)**

Questions to help guide you:

1. How do you want to be remembered for your emotional health? List three ways you want to leave a legacy in the area of emotional health. (Ex. I want to be remembered by others for (1) being happy and full of the Joy of the Lord, (2) being stable, one whom others can count on, (3) being vulnerable and real so others can learn from me.)

   _____

   _____

   _____

2. What are three things you can do to help achieve your three goals mentioned above? (Ex. I can smile at others when I see them. I can keep my word when I promise to call someone at a certain time each week. I can reply honestly when someone I trust asks if I am doing ok.)

   _____

   _____

   _____

Day 4: Physical Health

Memorize this scripture:

Praise the Lord! Blessed are those who fear the Lord, who find great delight in his commands. Their children will be mighty in the land; the generation of the upright will be blessed. Wealth and riches are in their houses, and their righteousness endures forever.
— Psalm 112:1-3 (NIV)

Questions to help guide you:

1. How do you want to be remembered for your physical health? List three ways you want to leave a legacy in the area of physical health. (Ex. I want to be remembered by others for (1) taking care of my body the way God intended, (2) being sober, (3) being strong and able to be physically active.)

   _____

   _____

   _____

2. What are three things you can do to help achieve your three goals mentioned above? (Ex. I will eat a serving of healthy vegetables each day. I will only drink nonalcoholic beverages. I will lift weights twice a week.)

   _____

   _____

   _____

Day 5: Financial Health

Memorize this scripture:

Stop collecting treasures for your own benefit on earth, where moth and rust eat them and where thieves break in and steal them. Instead collect treasures for yourselves in heaven, where moth and rust don't eat them and where thieves don't break in and steal them. Where your treasure is, there your heart will be also.
— Matthew 6:19-21 (CEB)

Questions to help guide you:

1. How do you want to be remembered for your financial health? List three ways you want to leave a legacy in the area of financial success. (Ex. I want to be remembered by others for (1) being careful with my finances and savings, (2) being a generous person as I am able, (3) giving my tithe to God.)

   _____
   _____
   _____

2. What are three things you can do to help achieve your three goals mentioned above? (Ex. I will save 10% a week from my paycheck in my savings account. I will save money so I can donate to a domestic violence shelter once a year. I will set aside money each week so I can give my tithe at church.)

   _____
   _____
   _____

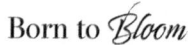

Day 6: Career and Serving Others

Memorize this scripture:

Timothy, in the presence of our great God and our Lord Jesus Christ, the One who is destined to judge both the living and the dead by the revelation of his kingdom—I solemnly instruct you to proclaim the Word of God and stand upon it no matter what! Rise to the occasion and preach when it is convenient and when it is not. Preach in the full expression of the Holy Spirit—with wisdom and patience as you instruct and teach the people.[1]
— **2 Timothy 4:1-2 (TPT)**

Questions to help guide you:

1. How do you want to be remembered for your career/service? List three ways you want to leave a legacy in the area of career and service. (Ex. I want to be remembered by others for (1) doing whatever I do in work as if I am doing it for the Lord, exceptionally, (2) being kind to each patron or person I serve, (3) continuing to learn and improve my skills.)

2. What are three things you can do to help achieve your three goals mentioned above? (Ex. I will give 100% of my effort at work each day. I will make sure my tone of voice is kind and that I smile. I will take a class in a new skill this year.)

Day 7: Sabbath Rest

Memorize this scripture:

Take the things you heard me say in front of many other witnesses and pass them on to faithful people who are also capable of teaching others.
— 2 Timothy 2:2 (CEB)

Do something to relax and restore yourself today! Meditate on God's promises. Go for a relaxing walk. Take a nap. Read a joy filled book. Call a friend.

Week 7: Inner Narration

Using what you have learned from this chapter, the scriptures you have memorized this week, and what you discovered while answering this week's questions, build on your original narration from earlier weeks and write an additional short godly narration using only positive words.

Additionally, take one sheet of paper and write a narration using all 7 weeks to create a completed godly narration about yourself.

Example: I am loved. I am pleasing to God. I am courageous and confident. I am consistent in pursuing my godly goals. I am kind to others...etc.

Conclusion

I am so thankful to my Lord, Jesus Christ, for healing me completely and allowing me the opportunity to walk this journey of healing with you! God is so good! He is faithful! Like the lotus flower—which was born to bloom and remained committed to pushing past the muck to arrive above the surface into the beautiful light, blossoming and living fully—you too, my friend, will rise above it all and fully blossom into the life God intended for you! Your story will bless many lives, and you will leave a lasting legacy of the great victory found through trusting in Jesus Christ! Your story will merge with the greatest story of all, which is the story of Jesus Christ and His great love and sacrifice for all! Your purpose and mission in life will be to help others come to know the great life found in Him.

If at any time you need an additional word of prayer, don't hesitate to call our ministry, YKI coaching, at 949-542-7166, or to email us your prayer request at info@YKIcoaching.com. Each and every one of us, including myself, need others to care for us and to encourage us here on this earth. If you need someone to remind you of your worth and to help you with your narration of who you are in Christ, my team and I are here for you! God has not asked you to take this journey of life alone. He has equipped you with His body, and we are here to serve you! God will give you the strength you need, and He will complete all He has in store for you, which is very, very good.

I love you my fellow believer, and I am praying for you! God bless you and keep you!

La Vonne Earl

Appendix

Born to *Bloom*

Feelings Chart

Appendix

Questions to Guide You in Discovering Your Feelings

Spirituality / Relationships / Emotional / Physical / Career & Ministry
(When discovering your feelings, take inventory on how you are feeling. Ask yourself these questions for each area of your life.)

1. How am I feeling spiritually? / Relationally? / Emotionally? / Physically? / Career & Ministry?

    _____
    _____

2. Where is that coming from?

    _____
    _____

3. Is it true?

    _____
    _____

4. What would I like to feel?

    _____
    _____

5. How can I get to that feeling?

    _____
    _____

6. Do I need to write? Pray? Read scripture? Sing? Go for a walk? Meditate on the desired feeling? Who can I ask to pray for me? Who can I pray for?

    _____
    _____

Replacing Negative Feelings or Lies One Has Believed with God's Truth

Below is a brief list of lies we often tell ourselves about who we are, and the truths that God says about who we are. Keep in mind the list is endless, and there are many more words that could be included. This is just a starting point.

The positive words are what you will use in creating the inner narrations that you are writing for yourself in the weekly activities in this book. You can use them even after you've finished this book as you continue in your life to focus on blessing yourself and others. Continue to add to the list as you grow in greater understanding of who were created to become. Everything good is from God and is your true identity in Christ.

Lies	**Truths**
Abandoned	Cared For, Cherished, Connected, Included
Abused	Adored, Cherished, Loved, Respected, Treasured
Accused	Absolved, Vindicated, Innocent, Understood
Afraid	Confident, Content, Peaceful, Powerful, Unafraid
Aggravated	Calm, Content, Happy, Peaceful
Agony	Comfort, Content, Healthy, Peaceful, Joyful
Alienated	Accepted, Cherished, Loved
Alone	Bonded, Cared For, Connected, Cherished, Loved
Aloof	Caring, Kind, Interested, Loving, Warm
Angry	Calm, Content, Forgiving, Loving, Merciful, Peaceful
Anxiety	Calm, Content, Faithful, In-Control, Peaceful, Powerful, Trusting
Apathetic	Caring, Compassionate, Concerned, Empathetic, Loving
Argumentative	Accepting, Agreeable, Flexible, Grace Filled, Harmonious, Peaceful
Arrogant	Accepting, Compassionate, Grace Filled, Humble, Loving, Teachable
Ashamed	Clean, Forgiven, Glorified, Powerful, Pure, Righteous
Attacked	Defended, Protected, Supported, Upheld
Avoidant	In Control, Dedicated, Facing, Helpful, Permitting, Purposeful
Awful	Content, Good, Happy, Joyful, Loving, Peaceful
Awkward	Bold, Confident, Content, Graceful, Smooth, Powerful
Bad	Good, Loved, Priceless, Treasured, Worthwhile, Valuable
Beaten Down	Elevated, Excited, Happy, Powerful, Purposeful, Joyful
Betrayed	Confident, Defended, Loved, Powerful, Protected, Respected, Supported
Bitter	Content, Forgiving, Loving, Peaceful, Purposeful, Useful
Blocked	Directed, Driven, Joyful, Passionate, Productive, Purposeful
Boastful	Grateful, Humble, Modest, Sincere
Bondage	Free, Liberated, Powerful, Released, Independent, Joyful
Bored	Creative, Excited, Passionate, Purposeful, Involved
Careless	Accurate, Attentive, Careful, Detailed, Thoughtful

Appendix

Chaotic	Calm, Methodical, Order, Organized, Peaceful, Purposeful, Quiet
Cheap	Cherished, Priceless, Treasured, Valuable, Worthwhile
Childish	Mature, Sensitive, Thoughtful, Understanding, Wise
Clingy	Content, Independent, Powerful, Self-Assured, Surrendered, Unattached
Closed-Minded	Accepting, Flexible, Humble, Teachable, Wise
Comparison	Adored, Assured, Content, Cooperative, Cherished, Independent, Unique
Complaining	Approval, Appreciative, Grateful, Thankful
Compromised	Faithful, Honest, Honoring, Loyal, Obedient, Steadfast
Compulsive	Accepting, Content, Flexible, Grace Filled, Peaceful, Relaxed
Conceited	Caring, Empowering, Grace Filled, Humble, Teachable
Conflict	Agreeable, Content, Forgiving, Peaceful
Controlling	Accepting, Flexible, Humble, Pliable, Relaxed, Submissive
Cynical	Accepting, Believing, Optimistic, Trusting
Confused	Clarity, Comprehend, Directed, Powerful, Purposeful, Wise
Deceitful	Honest, Honorable, True
Defeated	Successful, Victorious, Renewed, Tenacious
Deficient	Capable, Competent, Sufficient
Defiled	Clean, Purified, Renewed, Restored
Degraded	Dignified, Honored, Praised, Valued
Dependent	Capable, Independent, Self-Reliant
Depressed	Energized, Enthused, Excited, Joyful, Passionate, Purposeful
Despair	Assured, Courageous, Faithful, Hope Filled, Trusting
Despising	Caring, Faithful, Forgiving, Loving
Destroyed	Protected, Restored, Renewed, Saved
Different	Authentic, Equal, Equivalent, Kindred, Similar
Disappointed	Accepting, Content, Hopeful, Peaceful
Disappointing	Encouraging, Helpful, Pleasing, Satisfactory
Dumb	Bright, Intelligent, Smart, Wise
Egotistical	Humble, Selfless, Teachable
Embarrassed	Confident, Courageous, Proud
Empty	Filled with Joy, Full of life, Joyful
Enraged	Calm, Forgiving, Peaceful, Relaxed
Envious	Accepting, Charitable, Generous, Kind
Exhausted	Energized, Enthused, Invigorated
Failing	Accomplished, Capable, Competent, Successful
Faithless	Faithful, Loyal, Steadfast
Fearful	Brave, Courageous, Faithful, Trusting
Forced	Able to Choose, Free, Liberated
Forgetful	Able to Remember, Aware, Careful, Mindful, Thoughtful
Forgotten	Included, Remembered, Treasured

Forsaken	Favored, Indispensable, Saved
Frantic	Calm, Collected, Relaxed
Frustrated	Content, Delighted, Pleased
Gloomy	Bright, Excited, Happy, Light-Hearted
Greedy	Charitable, Generous, Unselfish
Grieved	Comforted, Consoled, Healed, Restored, Soothed
Guilty	Absolved, Forgiven, Pardoned, Peaceful, Unashamed
Hard-Hearted	Caring, Loving, Meek, Soft, Tender
Hateful	Affectionate, Forgiving, Gracious, Loving, Sweet
Haunted	Protected, Safe, Secure, Sheltered
Heartbroken	Consoled, Comforted, Cheerful, Healed
Hesitant	Assertive, Eager, Enthusiastic, Productive
Hopeless	Assured, Faithful, Great Future, Trusting
Humiliated	Esteemed, Favored, Honored, Loved
Hurried	Easy Going, Organized, Relaxed
Hurt	Comforted, Forgiveness, Honored, Revered
Impatient	Accepting, Calm, Patient, Relaxed
Impossible	Believing, Faithful, Possible, Trusting
Impulsive	Aware, Mindful, Slow, Thoughtful
Inadequate	Adequate, Capable, Competent, Qualified
Inconsiderate	Concerned, Considerate, Kind, Loving, Thoughtful
Indecisive	Clear, Decisive, Directed, Resolute
Indifferent	Attentive, Concerned, Mindful, Thoughtful
Ineffective	Effective, Meaningful, Productive, Successful
Insane	Balanced, Competent, Sane, Stable
Intense	Accepting, Calm, Grace Filled, Peaceful, Relaxed
Intimidated	Assured, Calm, Confident, Reassured
Jealous	Accepting, Benevolent, Esteemed, Well Meaning
Lacking	Abounding, Complete, Enough, Sufficient
Lazy	Alive, Ambitious, Energized, Motivated
Left Out	Cared About, Embraced, Honored, Included
Less Than	Equal To, Esteemed, Important, Talented
Let Down	Built Up, Edified, Elevated, Hope Filled
Livid	Calm, Forgiving, Loving, Merciful, Peaceful
Lonely	Accepted, Comforted, Connected, Fulfilled, Loved
Longing	Accepting, Content, Hopeful, Peaceful, Trusting
Lost	Clarity, Directed, Focused, Found, Purposeful
Low Self-Esteem	Confident, Secure, Self-Assured, Sure, Upbeat
Lustful	Disciplined, Integrity, Moral, Pure, Self-Controlled
Lying	Authentic, Forthright, Honest, Trustworthy, Truthful

Appendix

Mad	Forgiving, Happy, Joyful, Loving, Peaceful
Manipulated	Discerning, Perceptive, Prudent, Thoughtful, Wise
Manipulative	Decent, Forthright, Genuine, Honest, Proper
Martyr	Cared for, Independent, Strong, Valued, Wise
Materialistic	Generous, Giving, Godly, Humble, Spiritual
Mean	Caring, Considerate, Gentle, Kind, Loving, Virtuous
Melancholy	Blissful, Cheerful, Delighted, Happy, Sunny
Misunderstand	Comprehend, Enlightened, Grasp, Understand, Wise
Misunderstood	Admired, Appreciated, Heard, Seen, Understood, Valued
Moody	Cheerful, Constant, Happy, Stable, Steadfast
Morbid	Caring, Good Natured, Healthy, Sane, Sound
Naughty	Agreeable, Behaved, Disciplined, Good, Obedient
Negative	Cheerful, Happy, Optimistic, Positive, Upbeat
Neglected	Attended To, Cared For, Cherished, Remembered
Negligent	Attentive, Aware, Caring, Thoughtful, Responsible
Nervous	Calm, Composed, Confident, Peaceful, Relaxed, Stable
No Good	Adored, Priceless, Valued, Special, Treasured
Not Enough	Exceptional, Important, Very Loved, Worthy
Novice	Excellent, Expert, Praise-Worthy, Proficient, Skillful
Numb	Alive, Energized, Invigorated, Passionate, Refreshed
Obnoxious	Agreeable, Charming, Delightful, Enjoyable, Pleasant
Obsessive	Balanced, Content, Healthy, Relaxed, Secure, Stable, Steady
Offended	Calm, Content, Peaceful, Satisfied, Secure, Thankful
Opinionated	Accepting, Compliant, Flexible, Pliable, Tolerant
Opposing	Helping, Like-Minded, Obliging, United, Willing
Outcast	Accepted, Friend, Honored, Included, Insider, Restored
Out of Control	Calm, Centered, Composed, Grounded, Self-Controlled
Over-Sensitive	Accepting, Confident, Forgiving, Resilient, Strong
Old	Healthy, Purposeful, Significant, Vital, Youthful
Pained	Comforted, Eased, Peaceful, Pleased, Soothed, Tranquil
Purposeless	Decided, Determined, Purposeful, Significant
Perfectionist	Accepting, Allowing, Forgiving, Grace-Filled, Loving,
Perplexed	Clear, Discerning, Directed, Knowing, Understanding, Wise
Persecuted	Acquitted, Exonerated, Forgiven, Pardoned, Welcomed
Pessimistic	Cheerful, Enthusiastic, Hopeful, Optimistic, Trusting
Powerless	Dynamic, Impressive, Mighty, Powerful, Strong
Prejudice	Accepting, Admire, Appreciate, Loving, Welcoming
Prideful	Contrite, Humble, Modest, Simple, Teachable
Quarrelsome	Good-Natured, Harmonious, Peacemaker
Quitting	Committed, Resolute, Steadfast, Uncompromising

Rage	Calm, Forgiveness, Kind, Love, Merciful, Peace
Refusal	Cooperative, Flexible, Soft, Teachable
Regret	Accepting, Content, Forgiveness of Self, Onward, Peace, Progressive
Resentment	Friendship, Forgiveness, Love, Peace, Unity
Ridiculed	Approved, Applauded, Commended, Praised
Rude	Considerate, Gracious, Kind, Sympathetic, Warm-hearted
Sad	Cheerful, Comforted, Healed, Joyful, Peaceful, Restored
Self-Conscious	At Ease, Confident, Self-Assured, Trusting-Self
Selfish	Caring, Charitable, Considerate, Generous, Selfless
Shallow	Deep, Essential, Meaningful, Purposeful, Worthwhile
Shameless	Chaste, Dignified, Modest, Quiet, Reserved
Shocked	Comforted, Renewed, Unaffected, Unshaken
Shy	Affectionate, Assertive, Friendly, Neighborly, Receptive
Sinful	Apologetic, Chaste, Contrite, Honest, Repentant, Virtuous
Sinking	Buoyed-Up, Elevated, Invigorated, Uplifted
Slave	Appreciated, Free, Independent, Liberated, Renewed, Saved, Valued
Stressed	Calm, Composed, Peaceful, Relaxed, Tranquil
Suicidal	Assured, Full of Life, Hopeful, Loved, Loving, Passionate, Purposeful, Trusting
Tempted	Committed, Devoted, Loyal, Steadfast, Strong, True
Threatened	Guarded, Protected, Safe, Secure, Sheltered, Treasured
Tired	Alert, Dynamic, Energetic, Spirited, Vigorous, Vital
Traitor	Committed, Dependable, Honest, Loyal, Steadfast, True, Virtuous
Ugly	Beautiful, Graceful, Handsome, Pretty, Lovely
Unappreciated	Acknowledged, Appreciated, Loved, Valued, Revered, Treasured
Unforgiving	Exonerated, Forgiving, Merciful, Loving, Tender, Understanding
Unproductive	Beneficial, Effective, Useful, Productive, Prolific, Successful
Unthankful	Blessed, Grateful, Happy, Joyful, Pleased, Thankful
Unsure	Certain, Clear, Confident, Convinced, Resolute, Sure
Useless	Effective, Good, Important, Useful, Worthwhile
Victim	Champion, On-Top, In-Control, Victorious, Triumphant
Void	Complete, Energetic, Filled, Full, Hopeful, Joyful, Passionate
Wallowing	Directed, Fulfilled, Focused-On-Good, Purposeful
Weak	Energetic, Firm, Healthy, Powerful, Resolute, Strong
Why	Direction, Faith, Hope, Powerful, Purpose, Strong, Trust
Worry	Assured, Calm, Faithful, Hopeful, Trusting
Yearning	Blessed, Content, Fulfilled, Grateful, Gratified, Satisfied

Appendix

Who I Am in Christ Scriptures

Adored	1 John 3:1	Helpful	Ephesians 4:32
Authentic	John 8:32	Holy	John 17:17
Beautiful	Ecclesiastes 3:11	Honorable	Romans 12:17
Brave	Philippians 4:13	Hopeful	2 Corinthians 5:6
Calm	Isaiah 43:2	Hospitable	1 Timothy 5:10
Capable	James 1:5	Humble	James 4:10
Caring	Galatians 6:10	Intelligent	James 3:13
Cheerful	1 Thessalonians 5:16–18	Inspired	1 Thessalonians 1:6
Comforting	2 Corinthians 1:3–4	Joyful	Psalm 5:11
Committed	Ruth 1:16–18	Kind	3 John 1:5
Compassionate	James 1:27	Leader	Psalm 18:43
Confident	Hebrews 4:16	Loved	John 13:34
Content	Hebrews 13:5	Loyal	2 Kings 18:6
Daughter	Galatians 3:26	Merciful	Psalm 30:4
Dedicated	Revelation 14:12	Modest	1 Timothy 5:2
Dependable	1 John 2:5–6	Motherly	John 15:12–13
Determined	2 Timothy 4:7	Non-Judgmental	Matthew 7:1
Disciple	Isaiah 50:4	Nurturing	1 Peter 5:2
Disciplined	1 Peter 1:13	Obedient	Isaiah 1:19
Discreet	Proverbs 8:12	Passionate	1 Peter 3:13
Edifying	Romans 15:2	Patient	Proverbs 14:29
Energetic	Romans 12:8	Peaceful	Proverbs 3:17
Faithful	Psalm 23:6	Persevering	Psalm 51:10
Flexible	2 Timothy 2:15	Persuasive	1 Corinthians 9:20
Focused	Psalm 91:14	Positive	Proverbs 18:20
Free	2 Corinthians 3:17	Powerful	2 Timothy 1:7
Friend	Proverbs 17:17	Prayerful	1 Thessalonians 5:17
Full of Light	Matthew 6:22	Prepared	Philippians 1:10
Full of Love	Philippians 1:9	Productive	Proverbs 21:5
Fun	Ecclesiastes 5:18–20	Protective	John 15:13
Generous	Psalm 37:21	Proud	1 Corinthians 1:31
Good	1 Timothy 4:4	Pure	Philippians 4:8
Grace-Filled	2 Thessalonians 3:18	Quiet	Exodus 14:14
Grateful	Psalm 66:8	Relatable	1 Corinthians 9:20
Great Listener	Exodus 19:5	Reliable	Proverbs 12:5
Grounded	Ephesians 3:17	Resourceful	Isaiah 41:10
Happy	Psalm 9:2	Responsible	1 Timothy 5:8
Hard-Working	Proverbs 10:4	Reverent	Titus 2:3

Romantic	Genesis 2:18	Tender	1 Peter 3:8
Royal	James 2:8	Thankful	Psalm 100:4
Self-Controlled	2 Peter 1:6	Thoughtful	Philippians 4:10
Selfless	Mark 12:33	Tolerant	Colossians 3:13
Sense of Humor	Proverbs 31:25–26	Transparent	Philippians 1:10
Servant	2 Timothy 1:3	True	3 John 1:3
Simple	James 5:12	Trusting	Proverbs 30:5
Skilled	Proverbs 16:16	Understanding	1 Kings 2:3
Soft	Proverbs 25:15	Victorious	Romans 8:37
Son	Romans 8:14	Virtuous	Proverbs 31:10
Strong	Philippians 4:13	Warrior	1 John 5:4
Successful	Romans 8:28	Wholesome	Ephesians 4:29
Supportive	Hebrews 10:24–25	Wise	Ecclesiastes 7:12
Sweet	Psalm 133:1		

A Salvation Prayer

Dear Lord Jesus, I come to You humbly and confess that I am a sinner. I believe You died for my sins and rose from the dead, so that I could be set free from my sins. Please forgive me. I turn from my sins right now. I believe that You are Lord and Savior, and I am asking you to be mine. Come into my heart and life right now. I want to trust and follow You. Thank You for forgiving me and giving me a new life, in You. Amen.

Appendix

A Sample Narration

If you are looking for ideas or inspiration to guide you in writing a new narration, here is an example of one. You will want to personalize yours so that it says things about you that are fitting for your own personal needs, your vision for what you'd like your future to be, and the new ways you want to see yourself. Remember, you can use the Who You Are in Christ list to help you create a narration like this one for yourself. Use I AM statements that are meaningful to you.

I AM connected to others. I am capable and able to relate to my friends and family, and to love them as God loves—unconditionally, patiently, and with the appropriate boundaries. I am so grateful that I am able to care for others and to provide for them.

I have healthy boundaries and great discernment when it comes to maintaining safe and healthy relationships.

I AM discerning and wise. Through God's help and provision, I have all the resources I need in order to accomplish my goals. I can lend and give time to other people in need in ways that help them accomplish their goals.

As I AM now handling my finances efficiently, I am able to budget, save and decorate my home in order to create a comfortable and warm environment. I am making wise decisions in order to create the life I dream of.

I AM loved, safe and at peace.

I feel energized. My passion for life is increasing, as is my purpose.

I AM becoming more successful in my career as I continue to put forth the effort needed to succeed. I have great clarity and vision. I am empowered, strong and victorious.

New possibilities are opening for me.... moment by moment.

I AM increasing in wisdom in all areas of my life, and I am able to bring truth to others. I am balanced, creative, and fulfilled.

An Example Narration for Godly Anchoring

Through godly anchoring, we are seeking to align our character with who Jesus Christ is and who He says we are. I am only these things because Jesus Christ, my Lord and savior, is the great I AM. He goes before me. He perfects me. It is because of Him that I have peace and complete wholeness. Remember that pride goes before a fall (Proverbs 16:18). We must be careful when we anchor ourselves to do so in Christ and to give all honor, praise, and glory to Him. This is why I capitalize I AM—it is recognizing who is causing me to become these things, Jesus Christ, the Great I AM.

The list you can use to create your anchoring narration is endless, as God has so many good things to bless you with! Continue to add to your narration as God gives you His words.

There may be times where you do not say the entire list, and that is okay. But consistency is key. Bless yourself in the Lord at least in the morning and at night before bed. Just a few words are all that are needed. Read through your entire list at least once a week and watch how it grows! God says that He who is faithful with little will be faithful with much! (Luke 16:10) Be faithful with the little words He starts you with, and He will continue to give you more!

Add to your list characteristics you would like to possess and proclaim them over yourself with confidence! Remember, God called Gideon a "Mighty Warrior" when he was hiding in the wheat threshing floor. This is how God blesses us into who we are to become! You will get used to this new way and begin to bless not only yourself into your true identity and character, but also will bless others around you into their true identity.

I like to place my essential oil on my bathroom sink along with my Godly Narration list. This way, I see it when I brush my teeth twice a day and can easily start reading the list as part of my habitual spiritual practice. When I was first learning this method of blessing myself through Christ into my healing and wholeness, I kept this list with me throughout the day. I added it to my phone and looked at it all day until I was well enough to just keep the habit of twice a day.

Here's an example of what my own narration looks like:

I AM a daughter of the King. I AM beautiful and loved. I AM a woman of strength and mighty valor, full of wealth and wisdom. I AM courageous. I AM completely healed and victorious because Jesus has redeemed me and my life.

I AM pure. I AM confident. I AM blessed beyond measure. I AM forgiven, and therefore I forgive others. I AM filled with God's love, which I freely give.

I AM wise and discerning. I have healthy boundaries that protect me and my family. I AM dedicated and loyal, flexible and moved by the Holy Spirit. I trust and know that God has great plans for me. I read and obey His Word, the Bible. I know my Heavenly Father has many things He wants to say to me and teach me. I AM a good listener, and I love to learn.

I AM hard-working and also able to rest. I AM balanced. I AM able to do all things through Christ who gives me strength. I AM creative and resourceful.

Appendix

I AM kind and gentle with others, full of God's grace. I AM a shining light to all around me. I AM generous to the poor and seek ways continually to bless others. I AM able to bless and pray for my enemies.

I handle my trials with grace, as I know God works everything out for my good. I AM filled with joy!

I AM very passionate about life, and the Good News of the gospel! I seek to share it with others. I teach with wisdom and kindness as loving instruction pours from my lips.

I watch over and protect my household. Love permeates my home. My children love the Lord, and they will forever stay close to Him and teach their children and grandchildren to love God.

I AM successful in all that I do. I AM relatable to others. I AM fun to be around. I laugh easily and bring out the good in others. I AM a great mom and my children love me.

I AM centered on Christ. I AM focused. I AM easy-going. I AM physically healthy and enjoy taking care of myself. I AM happy and at peace. I AM stable, and I have a sound mind.

I AM content in all circumstances. I AM grateful for all my blessings. I AM deeply loved by God, and I AM never alone.

Thank You, Jesus, for being with me every moment of the day! I love You, Lord.

Tony's Example Narration

Tony's list grew quite long, as he continually added to it as words came to mind about what he wanted to hear in his mind, feel and become. As he continued to meditate on these words and encourage himself with them, he learned to treat himself as a loving father would treat him if he had one here in this life.

Add good and godly words to your list as well. There are many words in the Appendix to give you ideas. Feel free to repeat the same words as needed.

I AM a son of the King. I AM loved. I AM cared for and cherished. I AM forgiven and free!

I AM completely healed. I AM whole. I AM well. I AM clean. I AM healthy. I care for my body, mind and spirit. I AM thoughtful and sober minded. I AM strong and courageous. I have a voice, and I speak it with kindness.

I AM loving. I AM balanced. I AM intelligent. I AM handsome. I have great integrity. I AM connected to others and I communicate well. I AM filled with peace, and I AM content with my life.

I AM a caring person. I AM filled with forgiveness. I AM teachable, and I AM a great listener. I AM centered on Christ. I AM focused. I AM a good person, and I AM loved. I AM respected.

I AM confident. I AM filled with purpose, and I AM productive and successful. I AM victorious.

I AM aware of Christ with me at all times. I AM in control of myself. I AM grateful for all I have been blessed with.

I AM understanding and accepting of others. I have healthy boundaries. I AM protective of myself and others.

I AM filled with faith. I AM redeemed, renewed and restored. I AM honored and praised. I AM encouraging and helpful to others. I AM full of life! I AM full of joy! I AM treasured and valuable. I AM unashamed.

I AM capable of living a great life! I AM discerning and wise. I AM optimistic and filled with hope. I AM loyal and honest. I AM triumphant in all that I do. I AM blessed. I AM grateful. I trust God to work everything out for my good. I AM provided for. I AM hard working, productive and successful.

Thank You, Jesus, for the life You have given me. I love You, Lord.

Appendix

Resources and References

Linda Roy's Ted Talk, "What trauma taught me about happiness." — Available on YouTube, https://youtu.be/IUw8z7laPuI

www.ingramcontent.com/pod-product-compliance
Lightning Source LLC
LaVergne TN
LVHW061253060426
835507LV00020B/2308